OVERKILL

THE GREATEST WAR & HOSTAGE RESCUE THE WORLD HAS EVER KNOWN

Romans 5: The Power of God unto Salvation

J. W. Walker

Copyright © 2016 by Joseph W. Walker, Jr. All rights reserved. Except as permitted under the United States Copyright Act of 1976, no part of this book may be reproduced, stored in a retrieval system, or transmitted in any form or by any means, electronic, mechanical, photocopy, recording or otherwise, without prior written permission of the copyright owner except in the case of brief quotations embodied in critical articles and reviews. Nor can it be circulated in any form of binding or cover other than that in which it is published and without similar condition including this condition being imposed on a subsequent purchaser.

ISBN: 978-0-9979323-0-0 (Paperback edition)
FIRST EDITION
SERIES: OVERKILL: THE GOSPEL IN ROMANS

Unless indicated otherwise all Scripture taken from King James Version and the Literal Translation of the Holy Bible
Copyright © 1976—2000
By Jay P. Green, Sr.
Used by permission of the copyright holder.

Cover design *"Death the King"* by J. W. Walker
Cover drawing: Gustave Dore - Death on the Pale Horse

To purchase this book in quantity for Bible Study Groups or Book Clubs, please call 1-800-405-4423

Euthus Publishing
5300 N. Braeswood blvd. Ste. 4151
Houston, TX 77096

CONTENTS

Introduction 1
The Setting 15
Flashback 1: The Breach, The Bondage 23
Sin the Conquering King 32
Death the Conquering King 41
Flashback 2: Sin Without Imputation 50
The Lawless Reign of Death 62
The Foreshadowing: Figure 75
A Type of Contrast 80
Proof 1: The Gift is Not Like the Offense 88
- Laying Hold of the Power of God! 93

Proof 2: Acquittal is Much Better than Condemnation 105
End of the Typology 118
Final Flashbacks 3: Law Empowers Sin 127
Flashback 4: Grace Over-kills 133
Appendix 141
- The Love of God 141
- The Powerful Strategy and Method of Rescue: 142
- A Law Before Moses? 145

End Notes 150

*To my fellow warriors in the Good Fight of Faith
to lay hold of Eternal Life,
which God, who cannot lie,
promised before the world began.*

Introduction

*"Think not that I am come to send peace on earth:
I came not to send peace, but a sword."*
— *Mat 10:34, LITV*

Who doesn't like a passionate love story? One that involves deception, hostility, slavery, murder, rescue, and forgiveness, is very hard to resist. The allure of such a story is even greater when it's not the product of fiction, but the recollection of actual, real life events.

Well, the story we are about to hear is the truth behind actual historical events.

These historical events, not only marked the time-line of human history forever, but also have profound effects upon the world of mankind until this day.

Spiritual Things

The events we will study in this letter to the Romans, are a mixture of natural and spiritual, seen with the natural eye, and invisible things. Yet each event was/is 100% factual, and their effects very tangible.

In the gospel of John chapter 3, Jesus taught the existence of a spiritual reality, just as real as what we see with our natural eyes. However, it takes the New Birth for men to see it. He likened those who are "born from above", to the wind, which we cannot see with our eyes, but are very aware of.

> Jesus answered and said unto him, Verily, verily, I say unto thee, Except a man be born again, he cannot see the kingdom of God...Marvel not that I said unto thee, Ye must be born again. The wind bloweth where it listeth, and thou hearest the sound thereof, but canst not tell whence it cometh, and whither it goeth: so is every one that is born of the Spirit. —Joh 3:3-8

Since we born-again Christians have new eyes to see the unseen, let us use them to see the things Paul was inspired to reveal.

> Now we have received, not the spirit of the world, but the spirit which is of God; that we might know the things that are freely given to us of God. Which things also we speak, not in the words which man's wisdom teacheth, but which the Holy Ghost teacheth; comparing spiritual things with spiritual. But the natural man receiveth not the things of the Spirit of God: for they are foolishness unto him: neither can he know *them,* because they are spiritually discerned...For who hath known the mind of

the Lord, that he may instruct him? But we have the mind of Christ. —1Co 2:12

Why I Wrote This Book

Considering all the commentaries and books on Romans, why would I feel the need to write this book, and what qualifies me to write it?

Every good student should become an expert teacher *(Heb. 5:11-14)*. **In fact, that's the express definition of teaching—one expert creating another expert.**

Over the past 30 years, I have had the privilege of learning under very good Bible teachers. I have been compelled by what I consider *the spiritual gift* of teaching, to learn as much as I can about *The Faith*. My library of teaching books has steadily increase over the years, to include commentaries on Bible books, and scholarly works on subjects like textual criticism.

After teaching the letter to the Romans for a few years, I discovered, most of my commentaries contradict the Greek Word Studies on exactly **what** the text of chapter 5 was **saying**. Their contradiction was easy to miss, however, it effected the interpretation and meaning of the chapter.

From that point on, I learned the best method of determining what the Bible **means,** is to first be sure you know what it **says**—basic grammar before interpretation and application. (When you have "ears to hear"—so to speak—what it **says**, the Bible comes alive.) Because of this discovery, much of what this book shares will be fresh for even those readers who are already familiar with Romans.

Skepticism

Resistance to an unfamiliar interpretation of scripture is understandable, and a sign of a good Bible student. The Berean Christians in Acts 17 were examples for all Christians, because they searched the scriptures to see if what the apostles were teaching was true.

My request is that you follow their example completely, and before dismissing this unfamiliar interpretation of Romans, "search the scriptures" to see if what you hear is in fact true.

Although my emphasis on the allegorical, metaphorical, language of war and bondage may be different from anything you have heard on this chapter, the interpretation is not unique—as you will see—it is consistent with popular Greek word studies, and commentaries[1].

It takes discipline to not just accept your favorite teacher's interpretation of a passage, but to research it, as if you are hearing it for the very first time. Or, like the Bereans—as if you are being taught something questionable. In my 30 years of Bible study, I have found that many commentaries follow tradition, and as a result repeat errors of interpretation.

I'm not asking for an open mind, I'm asking for an eagerness to investigate the word of God.

> These were more noble than those in Thessalonica, in that they received the word with all readiness of mind, and searched the scriptures daily, whether those things were so. —Act 17:11

That there is war on planet earth,

Along with all of its consequences, (including evil, death, slavery, and continued hostility), is a fact confronting us in the first few pages of the Bible:

> And I will put enmity [hostility, hatred] between thee and the woman, and between thy seed and her seed; it shall bruise thy head, and thou shalt bruise his heel. —Gen 3:15

In this verse we read a promise from God Almighty to the serpent, that there will be war. He himself would put hostility between the serpent and the woman, and that hostility would lead to war. With such a beginning, it is no surprise we are immersed in the drama of wars throughout the Bible:

> "And I saw heaven opened, and behold a white horse; and he that sat upon him was called Faithful and True, and in righteousness he doth judge and make war." —Rev 19:11

So, if it begins and ends with war, it is reasonable to consider the story of the entire Bible a tale of war.

The New Testament of the Bible makes a shift away from the many wars between the nations in the Old Testament, to battles of a spiritual nature:

> "...For we wrestle not against flesh and blood, but against principalities, against powers, against the rulers of the darkness of this world, against spiritual wickedness in high *places*. Wherefore take

unto you the whole armor of God,..."
—Eph 6:12

In light of these truths, it is no wonder the gospel in Paul's letter to the Romans is also immersed in a drama of war.

Difficulty In Studying Romans

Before we begin our study of this drama, let's acknowledge the difficulty we will face. The subject we are about to study from the book of Romans is one which has been considered by many to be too complicated for the average Christian, and is often watered down, and skimmed over for Sunday school and group study.

We have at least two major themes presented in the first eight chapters of the letter:

1. Mankind's legal guilt before God, the wrathful Judge, seen in words like wrath, justification, condemnation.

2. The necessity and benefits of faith, demonstrated in the popular "Roman Road" for salvation verses: 3:10, 23; 6:23; 10:9-10, 13.

When you add the symbolism of war and bondage to the mix, the difficulty in interpretation is understandable. Not to mention the use of obviously metaphorical language throughout the letter.

However, Paul was inspired to write this letter to **new Christians** *(babes)* **in Christ**. So his message is fundamental to *every* Christian's understanding of the gospel. There's not a single hint in the letter that Paul expected his readers **not to understand** what the Spirit of God was moving him to write.

With that in mind, this book is meant for the average Christian. Its purpose is to make you stronger and smarter when it comes to the faith. The Bible teaches us: that we should grow in knowledge, from milk-drinking babes to mature adults, able to eat solid food *(Heb. 5)*. Therefore, I will do my best to not teach *over the head* of the average believer; but I will not **"water it down"**. My adult readers are likely all too familiar with lessons which teach as though you are not capable of understanding the deeper things of God.

> But God hath revealed them unto us by his Spirit: for the Spirit searcheth all things, yea, the deep things of God. —1Co 2:10

God didn't "dilute the potency of His medicine" when he inspired the writers of the Bible. God forbid we teachers fail to impart what He has given us, and water it down—effectively destroying its medicinal and nutritional value for transformation and spiritual growth *(Rom. 12:1-2, Eph.4:11-14)*.

This is done (I believe) mostly out of ignorance, and sometimes doubt—essentially saying: *Lord they are unable to understand the Word you gave me to tell them; I know better then you, and will water it down for them.* I have personally spoken with pastors and teachers who refuse to tackle difficult issues in the Bible, and as a result continue to teach things which are incomplete or untrue to their students.

Children and youth are naive due to inexperience with the reality of evil in this world—just observe them. They are consumed with ever-increasing sensual pleasures, and optimism for enjoying more. The letter of Romans is about world war that drafts into its ranks every soul born on this planet! Romans opens with the threat of God's wrath upon humanity and the power to escape that wrath. Romans 1-5 identifies powerful and deadly enemies. If you know that children's naïvety will leave them prey for predators in the neighborhood, what is your responsibility as the parent, guardian, Shepard?

> <u>I write</u> unto you, fathers, because ye **have known him** that is from the beginning. <u>I write</u> unto you, young men, because ye have overcome the wicked one. <u>I write</u> unto you, little children, because ye **have known** the Father. <u>I have written</u> unto you, fathers, because ye **have known** him that is from the beginning. <u>I have written</u> unto you, young men, because ye are strong, and **the word of God abideth in you**, and ye **have overcome** the wicked one. —1Jn 2:13

It is clear that the key to overcoming evil in this world is *knowledge* of the word of God!

It is interesting to note that, after the writer of Hebrews reprimanded the church for not being able to understand the things he wanted to share about Jesus and Melchisedec, he went on to serve the meat anyway, starting with Hebrews 7.

Let's let God determine what is too complicated for the young Christian.

A word to the teacher: What it means to be an ambassador

Paul opens his letter with:

> Paul, a servant [slave] of Jesus Christ, called to be an apostle [delegate, am-

bassador], separated unto [set apart for some purpose] the gospel of God,
—Rom 1:1

It is clear from Paul's opening sentence that he is **only** delivering to the Romans the message he was **entrusted with** from the Lord Jesus—the message is not his to alter in any way. This attitude and understanding is true of every faithful servant of the Lord. Let us follow in their steps.

Where the title comes from

Overkill is the use of *excessive force* or action that goes further than is necessary to achieve its goal. It implies that while the goal was accomplished, there was *collateral damage* as a result.²

I am using the word metaphorically to describe the excessive force suggested in chapter 5, as it compares the affect of Adam on the human race, with the greater effects of Jesus on the human race. Verse 20 is especially graphic as it states:

> But then Law came in, [only] to expand *and* increase the trespass [making it more apparent, and exciting opposition]. But where sin increased and abounded, grace [God's unmerited favor] has surpassed it and increased the more and super-abounded.
> —*Amplified Version*

The idea is, that as Sin conquered and reigned as King, it was in turn conquered by an even greater King—Grace "over-conquered" the great conqueror. Hence, **overkill**—in the sense of **over-conquer**.

This title is of course an attempt at being clever, and is by no means meant to be a completely accurate translation. Although, as you can see, the emotional and psychological impact of the word *overkill* matches what I believe to be intended by the word "superabound"— it is devastating, **excessive force!** In the words of another author: John Owen: the murderous effects of the work of Christ is "The death of Death".

Bondage

The first hint of bondage is in that first sentence of the letter: Paul is a "slave" of Jesus Christ. He makes it clear that he belongs to Him—does his bidding. So the setting of his letter from the start, is one of the Lord and his slave/ambassador. Although Paul's purpose is obviously to let his readers know from the beginning, that he is not contacting them for his own reasons, but has been sent by the Lord Jesus himself, with a message for them. This introduction nonetheless reveals important information to these new believers about the Lordship of Jesus Christ, and his kingdom: He is the master, and he has slaves/servants—Paul is one of them.

The series title and subtitle of this book comes from Paul's language at the beginning:

> For I am not ashamed of the gospel of Christ: for it is the power of God unto **salvation** to every one that believeth; to the Jew first, and also to the Greek. —Rom 1:16

This statement tells us, the entire mission of the Good News is one of deliverance, rescue, or salvation. This is where the idea (fact) of bondage in the book's title comes from.

Frequent Mistakes

Most of the commentaries I've read on Romans make a few mistakes in fundamental interpretation. This is more frequent in chapter 7, where there is much confusion on whether Paul is speaking as a believer, or before his conversion (unbeliever.) *(We will clear this up when we get there; it's not as hard as it appears.)*

I aim to avoid the following common mistakes:

1. Forgetting we are studying a letter with a logical progression of teaching. When we learn any new subject, we start with the basics, and then add to that foundation until we have completed building the intended structure—Romans does the same.

Romans is not a "book" with separate and isolated chapters. Paul's readers are taught the principals of the gospel starting with the fundamentals, and then building upon them. Therefore, we can be certain (in this letter) Paul doesn't intend his readers to forget chapters 1-3 when they get to chapter 5. Ignoring this fact has caused bible teachers to literally contradict earlier teaching when they interpret chapters 5-8. You can easily test my observation by seeing how many (or few) commentaries reference chapters 2-3 when they interpret chapters 5, 6 & 7. **This is a serious mistake!**

2. Failing to recognize patterns/ train of thought in teaching.

For example, Paul usually states the doctrinal truth, then explains the details related to the truth. The details never contradict the truth they are designed to explain. This principal is often violated in Romans 2, where Paul's intent is to prove that all men are deserving of God's wrath.

> For the wrath of God is revealed from heaven against all ungodliness and unrighteousness of men, who hold the truth in unrighteousness; —Rom 1:18

> And thinkest thou this, O man, that judgest them which do such things, and doest the same, that thou shalt escape the judgment of God? —Rom 2:3

> ... for we have before proved both Jews and Gentiles, that they are all under sin; As it is written, There is none righteous, no, not one:—Rom 3:9

By ignoring the train of thought, many people will mis-interpret chapter 2 to teach **we earn eternal life by good works.**

> Who will render to every man according to his deeds: To them who by patient continuance in well doing seek for glory and honour and immortality—eternal life: But unto them that are contentious, and do not obey the truth, but obey unrighteousness—indignation and wrath...—Rom 2:6-8

Following the train of thought, we learn these verses are only intended to show that righteous deeds are the only way to "earn" heaven, and unrighteous deeds earn God's wrath, but, "no one does righteous deeds — "no not a one'!

As Bible students our guide should always be:

> "Whom shall he teach knowledge? and whom shall he make to understand doc-

trine? them that are weaned from the milk, and drawn from the breasts. For precept must be upon precept, precept upon precept; line upon line, line upon line; here a little, and there a little:" —Isa 28:9

So, we should follow the train of thought, and expect to grow in knowledge and understanding toward the deeper things of God as we progress.

- So remember, we are studying a letter that is teaching young believers, starting with the basic foundation, and each truth is built upon the other. A good way to check your interpretation is: does it contradict anything taught earlier in the letter.

- Also, we should expect our instruction to move from simple to complex, and milk to meat, as we learn. In Romans this progression from milk to meat *seems* very fast, because Paul uses *symbolic language* to teach each part of the gospel. However, you will see that chapter 5 is actually elaborating on teaching already presented in the first 4 chapters, so what appears to be "meat" in chapter 5 is actually a part of the same meal we've already been eating—so to speak.

The First 4 Chapters?

Instead of reviewing the previous chapters up front, we will jump right into the drama in chapter 5, and let the text guide us back to earlier teaching when necessary. With this method we won't lose pace and should cover most of the letter up to chapter 6 by the time we finish this book.

A Prayer for Spiritual Sight

My prayer is that Paul's prayer to God for **spiritual** knowledge and revelation be realized in a measure by all of us believer's through this study of his letter to the Romans.

> Eph 1:16 Cease not to...mention of you in my prayers; That the God of our Lord Jesus Christ, the Father of glory, may give unto you **the spirit [not fleshly] of wisdom and revelation** in the knowledge of him: The eyes of your understanding being enlightened; that ye may know what is the hope of his calling, and what the riches of the glory of his inheritance in the saints, And what is the exceeding greatness of his power to us-ward who believe, according to the working of his mighty power, Which he wrought in Christ, when he raised him from the dead, and set him at his own right hand in the heavenly places...And hath put all things under his feet...

Let's get started!

The Setting

...Or again, how can anyone enter a strong man's house and carry off his possessions unless he first ties up the strong man? Then he can plunder his house.
—Matt 12:29 NIV

For I am persuaded, that neither death, nor life, nor angels, nor principalities, nor powers, nor things present, nor things to come, Nor height, nor depth, nor any other creature, shall be able to separate us from the love of God, which is in Christ Jesus our Lord.
—Rom 8:38f

Paul's Audience

It is helpful to remember that Paul is writing to new Gentile Christians, who were mostly in the dark when it came to God's revelation through the Old Testament prophets (including John the Baptist), who were sent only to the Jewish nation.

Overview: We Begin With the End

In Romans 5, verses 1-11 we reach a point in the letter where all believers have been granted access into a **state** of grace and peace with God *through* the Supreme Ruler, Jesus Christ.

> **Rom 5:1** Therefore being justified by faith, we have peace with God through our Lord Jesus Christ: By whom also we have **access** by faith **into** this grace wherein we stand, and rejoice in hope of the glory of God.

The spiritual reality pictured here is a restful and joyous destination reached…it is the end of a journey. We have trusted the gospel that the key of faith will open the way through the golden door into grace and God's glory (the glory we had previously "fallen short of". *Rom. 3:23*)

So, like many good movies, **chapter 5 begins with the happily ever after ending,** before we *flashback* to see how this joyous celebration came about.

When we look closer, we discover that the first two verses of chapter 5 are an exact parallel to chapter one:

> For I am not ashamed of the gospel of Christ: for it is the power [force] of God unto [leading to] salvation [rescue/safety] to everyone

that believeth; to the Jew first, and also to the Greek. For therein is the righteousness [justification] of God revealed from faith to faith: as it is written, The just shall live by faith. For the wrath of God is revealed from heaven against all ungodliness and unrighteousness of men, who hold the truth in unrighteousness; —Rom. 1:16-18

Chapter one can be seen, as Paul the ambassador, being sent by the Lord Jesus to God's beloved, to make a declaration of war and rescue;; He's not ashamed or intimidated by anyone one or anything he nay encounter, because he has been entrusted with the power of God Almighty. That "force of God" is "unto" salvation. The picture is a powerful force given to those who believe to get them somewhere—to safety/salvation.

Chapter five is the demonstration/realization of that power in the greatest war and hostage rescue this world has ever known. (The presentation of the gospel is a declaration of war and rescue to those you don't even know they are engaged in a war, or that they are prisoners. They have long ago surrendered to Sin, accepted Death as normal—and are oblivious to the reality of impending judgment day and God's wrath. The gospel of Christ is the power of God Almighty to deliver from this condition.)

Let's see the parallel between these two chapters.

- Both passages identify the believer, us who have FAITH, as the ones to whom this power of God is available.

- This force or power of God is utilized specifically to JUSTIFY, or make sinners RIGHTEOUS. It delivers the ungodly from God's WRATH, it accomplishes them: PEACE WITH GOD.
- This power of God produces faith, maintains the entire life of the believer: "for the just shall live by faith" (chp. 1). Because "no one seeks God," and "we were enemies" before he loved us and Christ died for us (chp. 5). Instead of "holding down the truth in unrighteousness" we live our lives by confidence in God's word. (chp. 1)
- "This power of God unto salvation, safety, rescue (chp. 1)" opens for us "access into this grace wherein we stand and rejoice in hope of the glory of God (chp. 5). It, by force, restores the glory we had fallen short of.

There we have this remarkable parallel between Romans 1:16-18 and 5:1-2 — **power declared in chapter one, and power demonstrated in five!** (This parallel is so remarkable, I see it as a strong indication of Divine inspiration. Because it seems extremely unlikely Paul could have such a grasp on this new spiritual information, recall this information, and write it in separate sections without a detailed outline before he wrote this letter. But under inspiration it's possible.)

The Love of God and Our Hero, Jesus The Lord!

We are told **the motivation** for God using his power/might/force to save us is His LOVE. Paul addresses his letter *"to all* *those who are in Rome, beloved of God, called to be saints."* His assignment is the get them to safety, to bring them home! This is a powerful story of love and war!

Verses 1-11 of chapter 5 tell us that "God's love is shed abroad in our hearts", he offered his son, and Jesus willingly gave his life for us.

The love of God for those **captives** He has set His love upon, like two gates, one in, and the other out of a city, opens and closes this dramatic teaching on the gospel of salvation in Romans chapters 5-8.

Proving the love of God is the overriding purpose of the truth revealed in these chapters. That overriding doctrine is: THE POWERFUL, SAVING, PROTECTING, DEFENDING, LOVE OF GOD for believers is beyond doubt.

Notice how seamless these "gates" work together to open and close the drama:

> Rom 5:5 And hope maketh not ashamed; because the <u>love of God</u> is shed abroad in our hearts by the Holy Ghost which is given unto us. For when we were yet without strength, in due time <u>Christ died for the ungodly</u>...But <u>God commendeth his love</u> toward us, in that, while we were yet sinners, <u>Christ died</u> for us. Much more then, being now justified by his blood, we shall be saved from wrath through him. For if, when we were enemies, we were reconciled to God by the death of his Son, much more, being reconciled, we shall be saved by his life. And not only so, but we also joy in God

through our Lord Jesus Christ, by whom we have now received the atonement... Rom 8:31 What shall we then say to these things? If God be for us, who can be against us? He that spared not his own Son, but delivered him up for us all, how shall he not with him also freely give us all things? Who shall lay any thing to the charge of God's elect? It is God that justifieth. Who is he that condemneth? It is Christ that died, yea rather, that is risen again, who is even at the right hand of God, who also maketh intercession for us. <u>Who shall separate us from the love of Christ?</u>...Nay, in all these things we are more than conquerors through him that loved us. For I am persuaded, that neither death, nor life, nor angels, nor principalities, nor powers, nor things present, nor things to come, Nor height, nor depth, nor any other creature, shall be able to separate us from the <u>love of God, which is in Christ Jesus our Lord</u>...

There you have it my friend, the sum total of all the teaching in Romans chapters 5-8! Those are the bookends which hold together all the truths contained between them. Is this not a powerful love story?

So now we know how the drama begins and ends—it ends exactly where it began. Logic tells us, that everything written in between, leads us to the final conclusion, which is: the believer's assurance of the powerful love of God.

If we know this drama is a love story; one of captivity, war, and heroic rescue, then we are likely to interpret this sacred drama correctly. I emphasize this, because these considerations are often ignored when studying and teachings these chapters—especially chapters 6 and 7, where guilt and insecurity are often emphasized.

The Powers That Be

Inside these bookends of God's love, we are about to meet three of those formidable enemies Paul had in mind at the end of chapter 8 when he asked: *"who shall separate us from the love of God...".* At the end of this story he was able to look around—as it were—after observing the defeat of these three enemies by the power of God, and ask: **who else is left between us and the God who loves us?!**

As we will see, those three enemies are Sin, Death, and The Law.

With this knowledge, we can safely say that nothing in chapters 5, 6, 7, or 8, is designed to discourage or dismay the true **believer,** who has been granted *"access by his faith into this grace in which we stand."* On the contrary, we will be convinced that the God of the universe loves us, and Jesus Christ REIGNS supreme, and has, (motivated by love), CONQUERED ALL! Chapter 5 is the beginning of the celebration of the gospel's benefits to those who believe, and the celebration explodes in the final verses of chapter eight.

Albeit, that earth-shattering rescue was hard fought!

Now let's visit the details of this mighty conquest and rescue.

Chapter Summary

- The main setting of our drama is found in the first two verses of the chapter: *Rom 5:1 Therefore being justified by faith, we have peace with God through our Lord Jesus Christ: By whom also we have access by faith into this grace wherein we stand, and rejoice in hope of the glory of God.*

- Through faith in Jesus, we have been granted peace with God, and access into the realm of grace. In this state, we are rejoicing in hope of the glory of God we had previously "fallen short of" *Rom. 3:23*. So, our study begins with the glorious end of a journey, before it flashes back to the difficult battle fought to reach this destination.

- There is a remarkable parallel between Romans 1:16-18 and 5:1-2 — **the power of the gospel is declared and that power demonstrated to rescue the faithfull to safety!**

- **Proving the love of God is the overriding purpose of chapters 5-8.** The overriding doctrine is: THE POWERFUL, SAVING, PROTECTING, DEFENDING, CONQUERING LOVE OF GOD THROUGH CHRIST for believers is beyond doubt. Romans 5-8 are meant to drive this truth home. Comparing Rom. 5:5-11 with 8:31-39 makes this truth very clear.

Flashback 1: The Breach, The Bondage

> **Wherefore, as** by one man sin entered into the world, and death by sin; and so death passed upon all men, for that all have sinned
> —Rom. 5:12

"Wherefore as..."

Wherefore, ties this section to what has just been discussed, by signaling conclusions are about to be made. "In light of what I have just established, I will now elaborate."

This simple observation is important, because any interpretation which fails to refer back to previous information is going to be faulty. And we will see as we go on, that Paul touches on facts shared since the beginning of his letter, not just the immediate context.

Connection to Context:

What we didn't learn from the first part of the chapter (vv. 1-11) is *how we became* slaves and fighters for the enemies of God.

- Paul began this letter by telling us that God is very angry with all men, and the gospel is the means of rescue from His wrath/punishment. (Rom. 1)
- He then proved by our conduct, that all men are sinners deserving of God's wrath. (Rom. 1-3)
- After that, he proved that righteousness (just standing before God the judge of all men's deeds), can only come by grace, through faith—not works. (Rom. 4)
- Then, in 5:6-11 he reiterated our sinful, spiritually weak, even hostile disposition, when God loved and rescued us through faith; proving our salvation wasn't because of our good deeds.
- Now he is about to tell us: *how* we got ourselves into that dangerous predicament of God's wrath and condemnation, and why power is needed to save us.

In this flashback, he will fill in important details about our former condition—namely our bondage—which required not only a change of our minds and hearts, but powerful force from God for deliverance from bondage and slavery.

Flashbacks

If we view v. 1 like beginning a movie or drama starting with a scene from the end of the story. Then, here in verse 12, the movie cuts to some **earlier point in time** in a **"flashback"**:

> *A flashback or analepsis is an interjected scene that takes the narrative back in time from the current point in the story.[3] Flashbacks are often used to recount events that happened before the story's primary sequence of events to fill in crucial back story.[4]*

Romans 5:1-11 is the "primary sequence" in time. The glorious state described in verse 1 is **the present reality** accessed by faith; it is the end of the journey away from God's wrath, into the salvation, promised in chapter one. Through faith in the gospel, a state of freedom, peace and joy is reached.

Verse 12 is a FLASHBACK to fill in **crucial back story**: Details which identify the enemy and glorify the hero—the *Lord* Jesus Christ. A proper understanding of the **power of God** manifested in the Lord Jesus' conquest is important for our understanding—we are transformed by renewing our mind (Rom. 12:1-2). It also helps us appreciate the love of God demonstrated in saving us from bondage and granting us access into this state of grace.

Remember how Paul began his letter:

> For I am not ashamed of the gospel of Christ: for it is the power of God unto salvation to everyone that believeth; to the Jew first, and also to the Greek.
> —Rom 1:16

Now he is about to demonstrate **the power of God** through historical events. Up until now he has demonstrated that faith is God's only method for saving men. Now, he will **demonstrate the POWER of God and Christ** which makes this method of salvation possible.

... **"As"** is an adverb which means: *just as, exactly like.*

"Wherefore as" begins the comparison designed to prove the conclusions made about Jesus in the previous verses.

Some commentators say that Paul begins to compare Adam and Jesus but goes off and picks the comparison up again in vs. 15. So, with that interruption the flow of thought would be something like this:

> Wherefore, as by one man sin entered into the world, and death by sin and so death passed upon all men, for that all have sinned:... For if through the offence of one many be dead, much more the grace of God, and the gift by grace, which is by one man, Jesus Christ, hath abounded unto many.—Rom 5:12,15

However, I believe the second part of the comparison, i.e. Jesus, was already established:

> And not only so, but we also joy in God ***through*** our Lord Jesus Christ, ***through*** whom we have now received the atonement.
> — Rom 5:11

So, Adam is actually the second part of the comparison. Paul has just declared that we were in a terrible condition when God loved us—Jew and Gentile; Jesus died for us **all** and we are **all** assured of escaping God's wrath through him.

So, now he adds the other side or second part of the comparison *(wherefore as)* to prove his point, by taking us back to the father of the entire human race—Adam; The man who allowed the reign of Sin and Death.

...by...

Action Words, Our Road Map

This sections (vv. 12-21) is also tied to the preceding by the important prepositions *"in"* and *"by/through"*. These words are extremely important, because they tell us where the drama is moving at that moment in time.

Through (a prepositional verb) **is used in almost every verse of this chapter (19 times in 21 verses).** This highlights a definite pattern. Because Paul repeatedly uses the prepositional verb "through", we know that he is continuing a train of thought. Repetition is one of the Bible's methods of teaching and emphasizing important points.

Dia (see chart on next page) describe a **path taken**, by (through) a certain channel. *En* points to **a position** in space, or a destination reached.

For example, in verse 1 the starting point (ek) is faith, destination reached is into **(eis)** this realm of *grace wherein* **(en)** *we stand*; and the channels **through (dia)** which this destination is reached is Jesus Christ.

28 | Overkill: Romans 5..

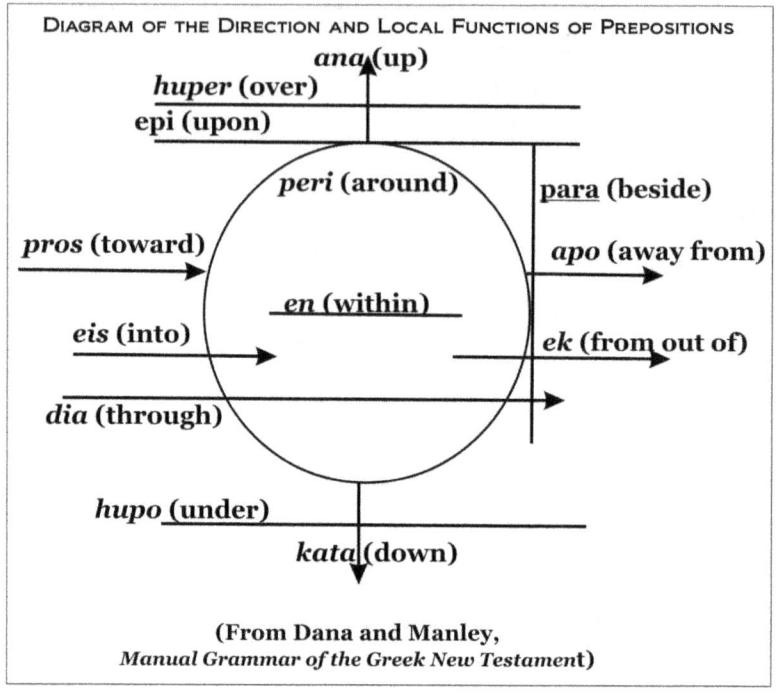

(From Dana and Manley, *Manual Grammar of the Greek New Testament*)

FAITH>>--J̶E̶S̶U̶S̶→PEACE & GRACE

Therefore being justified by *[ek: out from, the source]* faith, we have peace with God **through [dia]** our Lord Jesus Christ: **By** *[dia: through]* whom also we have access by faith into [eis] this grace wherein [en] we stand, and rejoice in hope of the glory of God. —Rom. 5:1

(By the way, this verse tells us what "from faith to faith" means in Rom. 1:17)

This distinction is very important because most commentaries on Romans chapter five interpret its *meaning* as if *in (en)* is the dominating verb, instead of *through,* as is the case. This mistake shifts the meaning, and allows for all kinds of misunderstanding. Passing **through** a thing is very different than being **in** a thing. Remember, in the Word of God not *"one dot or tittle"* is carelessly spoken.

So, we see proof in the constant use of "through", that our current drama (vv. 12-21) is actually a continuation of what has preceded it (vv. 1-11).

The entire chapter we are focusing on is clearly designed to give *details* about our salvation **through** Christ, and emphasize a central ingredient of the gospel: namely: Grace REIGNS *though* RIGHTEOUSNESS, **unto** ETERNAL LIFE, **THROUGH** one man: Christ our Supreme Ruler (5:11, 21).

Another way to appreciate the importance of the verb *through* in this chapter, is recalling Jesus' statement in John:

> Thomas saith unto him, Lord, we know not whither thou goest; and how can we know the way? Jesus saith unto him, I am the **way** *[road, path, means]*, the truth, and the life: no man cometh unto the Father, but *by* me.—John 14:5

Jesus is therefore the only road through which one passes to reach the Father. In our current passage he is the ***road through which one travels, or the means by which one travels*** away from the bondage of Sin, Death, and Condemnation, to ***reach*** righteousness, grace and eternal life.

"*Wherefore as by one man...***"** is the beginning of the proof for this assertion.

Chapter Summary

- This chapter covers the first of 4 flashbacks which begin in verse 12. A *flashback or analepsis* is an interjected scene that takes the story back in time to fill-in important details.

- The word "wherefore" lets us know that Paul is about to draw conclusions from what he has already taught since the beginning of the letter, and previous verses. So, if our study doesn't take us back to previous chapters we will be missing some important information.

- We were told that God loved us while we were His enemies. What we didn't learn from the first part of chapter 5 (verses 1-11), is *how* we became slaves and fighters for the enemies of God, and why we needed to make "peace with God." (Review the 5 bullet points on pg. 22.)

- In Romans 1:12 Paul declared that the gospel is the "power [force] of God unto salvation"; in chapter 5, through the use of flashbacks, he is showing us God's power in action.

- The comparison between Jesus and Adam began with Jesus in verses 1-11. We now flashback to Adam to magnify Jesus by comparison.

- Action words are our road map on this journey, . They tell us what direction the action is moving.

- The verb ***by/through*** is key: it is used 19 times in 21 verses. Most commentaries interpret this section as though the preposition "in" is used. (Review diagram on pg 28.) This error leads to misinterpretation.

- The entire drama is designed to show us what, and who we went "through" to gain "access into this state of grace in which we stand."
- Jesus our rescuer is the mighty hero of our story.

Sin the Conquering King

Jesus answered them, Truly, truly, I say to you, Everyone practicing sin is a slave of Sin. —John 8:34

Rom 5:12-14

Wherefore [for this reason], as [just as, even as] by [through] one man **Sin entered into the world** [cosmos], and Death by [through] Sin; and so [in this manner] Death passed [travel through a region] upon all [every] men, for that all [the whole] have sinned [missed the mark, erred]...

The Captivity **Through One Man**

Now, our attention is taken back in time, to the beginning of human history, to make an exact comparison with another man whose life influenced the entire human race in a similar way that Jesus has.

The idea that one man can pay for the *crimes* of the whole human race, is still hard to believe by opponents of Christianity. Apparently, it was a doctrine the Spirit of God led Paul to explain to the new gentile Christians at Rome.

So if you've ever been asked how *one man* could possibly die for *everyone else's* sins, you will find your logical and accurate answer here in Romans 5.

The key phrase is "as **through one man**". As we learned on page 27, there is a difference between the word through (dia) and in (en). The action here is *through* Adam, not *in* Adam. We are directed to visualize Sin passing through Adam.

Even as through Jesus comes reconciliation and life (vv. 10-11), through One man—Adam...

Sin entered into the world:

This is the first time in this letter that Paul obviously personifies (speaks of as possessing human characteristics) Sin, Death, and the Law. (This is a result of the Spirit's inspiration: the words of the prophet are not his own, but are God's —2Pet. 1:20,21). This point is very important to remember throughout our study of this and the next 3 books in this series. The Spirit of God obviously wants us to get a good picture of these truths through illustrations of human-type relationships, behavior, and characteristics. When we read the word "reign" we understand a ruler on a throne with power over men. I believe these pictures are CRITICAL to properly understanding the gospel truths in Romans. For this reason I will capitalize as nouns, Sin, Death, and Law, when they are personified.

Most teachers and commentators fail to make this distinction, and interpret these words as *adjectives and verbs,* when the context uses them as **personal nouns.**

So, let's look at what Paul says about the reign of Sin and Death—the kings. Through one man...

*Sin **entered into** [eis, pg 28] **the world**:*

> *Vincent's Word Studies:* **Entered into:** As a principle till then external to the world.
>
> *Robertson's Word Pictures:* Sin entered into the world. Personification of sin and represented as coming from the outside into the world of humanity.

The focus is Sin's *entrance into* the drama. If we accept the fact that "Sin" is a noun, not an adverb or adjective, there are two ways of understanding how it is used here:

1. Sin is a thing—like a disease or virus. It had the capacity to infect one individual, and through him spread to other human beings, essentially causing a global pandemic of sickness. This disease is 100% fatal, causing death to all—*Wherefore [for this reason], as [just as, even as] by [through] one man sin entered into the*

*world [cosmos], and death by [through] sin; and so death passed upon [**infected**] all men...*

2. Sin is an entity—like a king who was granted access into a territory through one man (a gate keeper), or a sovereign Ruler who turned over his power to Sin. Once in the territory, he subdued the watchman, and was powerful enough to *conquer* the rest of the inhabitants of the region.

We know the first option is true, because sin is a disease. The word is used in that way in Romans, and passages like:

> Husbands, love your wives, even as Christ also loved the church, and gave himself for it; That he might sanctify **and cleanse it with the washing of water by the word,** That he might present it to himself a glorious church, not having spot, or wrinkle, or any such thing; but that it should be holy and without blemish. So ought men to love their wives as their own bodies. He that loveth his wife loveth himself. For no man ever yet hated his own flesh; but nourisheth and cherisheth it, even as the Lord the church: —Ephesians 5:24-29 KJV

> Your glorying is not good. Know ye not that **a little leaven leaveneth the whole lump?** Purge out therefore the old leaven, that ye may be a new lump, as ye are unleavened. For even Christ our passover is sacrificed for us: Therefore let us keep the feast, not

with old leaven, **neither with the leaven of malice and wickedness; but with the unleavened bread of sincerity and truth.** —1 Corinthians 5:6-8 KJV

Knowing this, that our old man is crucified with him, that the **body of sin [diseased] might be destroyed,** —Rom 6:6

...But he was wounded for our transgressions, he was bruised for our iniquities: the chastisement of our peace was upon him; and with his stripes **we are healed**. All we like sheep have gone astray; we have turned every one to his own way; and the LORD hath laid on him the **iniquity** of us all. —Isa 53:5

We also know that the second option is true, because Sin is an intelligent entity in passages like these: *Rom 7:11 For Sin, taking occasion by the commandment, **deceived me**, and by it slew me. Rom 5:21 That as **Sin hath reigned** unto death...*

These two ways of understanding sin are used interchangeably throughout this section of Romans. So, careful attention has to be paid to get the sense the Bible intends. I mention this point, because one of my favorite Greek word studies (Wuest's) interprets sin exclusively as a disease (the sinful nature) in nearly every place it appears in this section of Romans—as you can see, this is a mistake that destroys the true meaning.

Compare Gen. 4:7, the **first mention** of sin in the Bible, where Sin is personified and depicted as a wild animal crouching *outside* of Cain's door.

> If you do well, is there not exaltation? And if you do not do well, Sin is crouching at the door; and its desire *is* toward you; but you should rule over it. —Gen 4:7

There is remarkable consistency between the record of Sin's first mention in Bible history, and the teaching in this letter to the Romans. Especially the relationship between Sin, Death and the Law of Moses.

Also Compare-

> Jesus answered them, Verily, verily, I say unto you, Whosoever committeth sin is the servant of Sin. —Joh 8:34

Here, Jesus subtly characterizes habitual acts of sin as an indication of personal slavery to Sin—personifying Sin as a master. Coming from the Lord, this wasn't just rhetoric—it is a spiritual fact; and as for slavery and labor, we know that Sins' wages to its servants is death (...the wage of Sin is death. Rom 6:23).

Sin is personified along with Death and the Law in this section so that Jesus Christ-the Lord, can be seen as the Great Rescuer, Deliverer, Conqueror and King!

To miss this point will certainly cause you to misinterpret the meaning and purpose in chapters 5-8.

So Sin *entered into* (not through, but into)...

the world *(inhabited world, cosmos).*

The word *world* is a translation of the Greek: kosmos (kos'-mos)

> **Strong's definition:** *Probably from the base of G2865; orderly arrangement, that is, decoration; by implication the world (in a wide or narrow sense, including its inhabitants, literally or figuratively [morally]): - adorning, world.*

It is a fact, that the entire created universe was pronounced by God in Genesis to be "very good". It is also a fact, that all that we can observe with our eyes, and scientists can test with instruments, is subject to erosion and ultimate death. The sun and entire universe is known by scientists to eventually erode and die. No wonder Sin is personified here, because it hasn't just affected the hearts of men, but has powerfully affected the entire cosmos. One man subjected all of creation to Sin; on account of which we must long for a new heaven and earth.

> For the earnest expectation of the creature waits for the manifestation of the sons of God. For the creature was made subject to vanity, not willingly, but by reason of him who has subjected the same in hope, Because the creature itself also shall be delivered from the bondage of corruption into the glorious liberty of the children of God. For we know that the whole creation groans and travails in pain together until now. — Rom 8:19 -22

And I saw a new heaven and a new earth: for the first heaven and the first earth were passed away; and there was no more sea.— Rev 21:1

Chapter Summary

Wherefore [for this reason], as [just as, even as] by [through] one man **Sin entered into the world** (cosmos), and Death by [through] Sin; —Rom 5:12-14

- This chapter covers the first major event in the first flashback: the entrance of Sin *into* the organized, inhabited world or cosmos.

- The focus or starting point of the action is Sin's entry point: "through one man". The focus of the action in verses 1-11 was *through* Jesus Christ we access "into this grace in which we stand". Now by way of contrast, the focus is taken back to Adam and what happened *through* him.

- This is the first time in the chapter that Paul personifies Sin. ***Robertson's Word Pictures:*** *Sin entered into the world. Personification of sin and represented as coming from the outside into the world of humanity.* The implication is that Sin's entrance was deliberate and intentional with the purpose of conquering.

- Sin is described as both a disease and personified as in human terms as an entity throughout Romans; a careful examination of the context will help our interpretation. Sin is personified along with Death and the Law in this section so that Jesus Christ-the man, can be seen as the Great Rescuer, Deliverer, Conqueror and King!

- "Sin entered into the world," (inhabited world, cosmos) includes all of the created universe. Romans 8:19-22 confirms this truth: all of creation suffers deterioration because of the one man's sin.

- The diagram on page 28 helps us follow the action. Sin went through Adam into the cosmos; as we shall see: spread like a disease and conquered all as dictatorial King.

Death the Conquering King

Gustave Dore, Death on the Pale Horse

And when he had opened the fourth seal, I heard the voice of the fourth beast say, Come and see. And I looked, and behold

> *a pale horse: and his name that sat on him was* **Death**, *and Hell followed with him...*—**Rev 6:7**

> Wherefore, as by one man Sin entered into the world **and Death by** [dia, through] **Sin; and so** [in this manner] Death passed upon all men,—**Rom 5:12**

P aul's flashback in history now introduces Death into the drama. Death (like Sin), is personified from this point on. It was through Sin that Death entered the cosmos. This historical fact is recorded in the book of Genesis. Adam and Eve caused death to the entire cosmos. (Compare Rom. 8;19-22)

Paul has now introduced two of the enemies Jesus had to triumph over to deliver believers into "this grace in which we stand".

So, Death entered the cosmos after and through Sin,

And So: *"in this manner"*[5]

> Barnes: And so—Thus. In this way it is to be accounted for that death has passed upon all people, to wit, because all people have sinned. As death followed sin in the first transgression, so it has in all; for all have sinned...And as all have sinned, so death has passed upon all people.

I agree with Barnes. All of the references show that the word *"so"* does not mean *therefore* (as a direct cause of), but, the word marks a comparison between two similar things, as in: "in this manner or fashion, likewise". The most probable meaning therefore is: In the same manner that Death followed Adam's sin, it follows everyman's sin. Or, Death has passed upon all men in the same way it did Adam—because all have committed sin. Sin always brings in Death after it.

If we (like some,) interpret "and so" to mean "therefore," we would interpret the meaning like this:

> "Sin entered through Adam and death through sin, **therefore** [as a result—not a comparison], death spread to all men, because if Adam sinned all sinned."

Adam's sin becomes the single occasion of all mankind's sin, instead of the **manner or pattern** for all mankind's sin, as "and so" properly describes. This could suggest: one sin equals death for all, instead of one sin lead to many of the same kind of sin and death.

Original Sin?

Many commentaries and teachers interpret this phrase as though it says "*therefore death spread to all men.*" They do this to support the teaching of **Original Sin**, The belief that all mankind sinned along with/in Adam's sin. They say "Adam represented all mankind as our legal/federal head—he stood for us, and his sin was therefore our sin, as we are considered *in his loins*.. As Jesus is our righteousness (we are righteous in him—we have no righteousness of our own), so Adam is our sinfulness and condemnation."

I disagree with that interpretation of this passage. It is contrary to the Bible's **clear** declaration in every passage dealing with sin, death, and judgment; i.e., every man must account for his deeds/works in the flesh! No one will be condemned for another's deeds. This is the clear record of the Bible from Genesis to The Revelation (Cp. Rom. 2:6, Matt. 16:27). Up to this point in the Bible, those who have been judged for their parents sins have also **repeated** those sins (John 8:39 cp. 1John 4:7-21). There has never been an innocent person condemned solely for their parent's sin.

> If thou doest well, shalt thou not be accepted? and if thou doest not well, sin lieth at the door. And unto thee shall be his desire, and thou shalt rule over him. —Gen 4:7

As proof of this point I would like to remind you that the first occurrence of the word Sin in the Bible is a noun. We find it crouching like an animal outside of Adam's son Cain's house (or heart). It's not pictured as residing in his heart! If he sinned in Adam, Sin would have been inside, and not seeking to possess him, but would have already occupied the house.

Objection!: What about David's sin of numbering Israel which resulted in the death of 70,000 men in 1Chr. 21? A careful reading of the preceding history will reveal that David's pride and obstinate heart was **a reflection of the spiritual condition of Israel-the nation** at that time, which provoked the Lord's anger and judgment. (*see 2Sam. 24*)

One of the strongest arguments against the teaching that every human sinned in Adam, is Jesus. He too was Adam's offspring, yet without sin. If sin were imputed to all men in Adam's loins, he could not have escaped it. Jesus was conceived by the Holy Spirit, (Adam was as well, having no earthly father or mother), they were both perfect. However, unlike Adam, Jesus was 100% obedient throughout his life. If original sin is true, Jesus would have been **born a sinner,** because his genealogy through his mother is traced back to Adam. (*Lk. 3:38*)

Death passed upon all men, because ALL HAVE SINNED

It is at this point most commentaries make their strongest argument for "original sin" and "imputation of sin, in Adam". They say, the phrase "all have sinned", in the original Greek grammar, is in the *aroist tense,* and therefore refers to one single, all encompassing act. Which they believe to be Adams sin. Robertson's Word Study says: "*This tense gathers up the whole race into one statement (a timeless aorist).*" They insist a different tense would have been used if the Spirit of God meant to refer to the *many acts of sin* committed by mankind.

However, this was an already proven fact, as Rom. 2:12 and 3:23 *use* the *identical phrase: "all have sinned"*. So, the aroist tense in both places stresses the *all encompassing fact*, proven by past <u>deeds</u>. History and current behavior prove all men do/ *have sinned* and therefore die. Men sin all the time, hence the use of aroist tense without a reference to any particular act of sin—including Adam's,—<u>the aroist stresses a undisputed fact!</u> Mankind's deeds prove this fact.

> Rom 2:12 For as many as ***have sinned*** without law shall <u>also perish</u> without law: and as many as ***have sinned*** in the law <u>shall be judged</u> by the law;

> Rom 3:23 For all ***have sinned***, and come short of the glory of God;

SIN entered the inhabited world ***though*** Adam, Death ***through*** Sin, and so as Death passed *into* Adam because of his sin; It likewise passed into all men, because all have in the same manner sinned (committed their own sin).

FACT: Sin entered **INTO** the world **THROUGH** Adam **not in** Adam. The picture here is not Adam as the *source,* but the *channel* through which Sin passed and infected others—causing death.

FACT: No hint of GUILT by association, or imputation, in the first three chapters of Romans, which are written to prove mankind's sin and guilt (see 3:9). The tense of the grammar is consistent with Paul's previous usage of the phrase "all have sinned". It is a documented fact, supported by the history of actual ungodly and unrighteous deeds of men. **Paul is not proving the *fact or existence* of sin in chapter 5, that has already been done (chps. 1-3); he is proving Sin's power and reign, and the power of God to defeat it through Christ!**

FACT: This verse does not support "sinned" as meaning corrupt nature! (Death passed upon all because all have a sinful nature received from Adam?) No, the *verb "sinned"* is <u>never</u> used in that way in this epistle. **It always describes action, not a characteristic or attribute; it is not an adjective, it is a verb.** (refer back to Rom 2:12, 3:23, also the following verses.)

> Nevertheless death reigned from Adam to Moses, even over them that had not ***sinned*** after the similitude of Adam's transgression, who is the figure of him that was to come. —**Rom 5:14**

> And not as *it was* by one that ***sinned***, *so is* the gift: for the judgment *was* by one to condemnation, but the free gift *is* of many offences unto justification. —**Rom 5:16**

So sinned interpreted as sinful nature is not accurate.

FACT: The only thing this verse says is that all of Adams offspring experience **Death,** because of, and in the same manner as Adam did; because like Adam they too have sinned. If any man doesn't sin, death could not reach him (Rom. 2:6-11). Hence, Jesus Christ (truly righteous) died for our sins, not his own (Gal. 1:4, John 10:15,18).

A More POWERFUL and PROFOUND declaration of the Gospel, declared by Jesus in John 3, and about to be expounded upon by Paul here, and in chapters 6-8, is, that Death has no claim on believers either, since the death of Christ, and the believers union with Him through faith!!!!

NEXT

The next **FLASHBACK** section will more fully explain the last clause ie. *"and so death passed upon all men, for that all have sinned"*. Paul takes us back in time, and points out certain details that are important to the teaching.

Final Summary

> Rom 5:12,15 Wherefore, as by one man Sin entered into the world **and Death by** [dia, through] **Sin; and so** [in this manner] Death passed upon all men, for [in the same manner] all have committed sin...

- Death is personified as an agent which entered the created universe through Sin.
- This flashback takes us back to the garden of Eden, to discover the point at which Sin and Death entered the world. It was through one man—Adam.
- **"and so"**; In the same way Death passed to all men, because all men have sinned. The emphasis is not the result of Adams sin, but the manner: In the same why Adam died due to personal sin, men die due to personal sin. This verse doesn't teach that everyone sinned "in Adam".

- The tense of the grammar is consistent with Paul's previous usage of the phrase "all have sinned" (3:23 *All have sinned and fallen short of the glory of God*).
- the *verb "sinned"* <u>**never**</u> means ***sinful nature*** in this epistle. **It always describes action, not a characteristic or attribute; it is not an adjective, it is a verb.**

Flashback 2: Sin Without Imputation

> (For until the law sin was in the world: but sin is not imputed when there is no law.
> —Rom 5:13

P aul has just stated, that like Adam, **Death passed to all men**, because all men **have sinned**.

Sin means to *err, transgress*; **suggesting** a violation of law, some standard, or a prohibition. However, as we have seen, the first chapter of Romans (18-20) reveals: **sin is also what I would call a** *"malfunction"*.

> For the wrath of God is revealed from heaven against all ungodliness and unrighteousness of men, who hold the truth in unrighteousness; Because that which may be

known of God is manifest in them; for God hath shewed it unto them. For the invisible things of him from the creation of the world are clearly seen, being understood by the things that are made, even his eternal power and Godhead; so that they are without excuse: —Rom. 1:18-20

In this statement, there is no violation of a specific prohibition. It describes *suppression of **innate** knowledge,* which should have guided men toward the correct path. Let's see what this means in our drama.

For until Law:

"For" indicates the beginning of an explanation of how Death passed upon all men because they sinned.

Strong's definition of *until*: (of time) *until* or (of place) *up to*: The word "the" is not in the Greek, it's simply *"until Law"*. However, the next verse makes it plain that The Law of Moses is intended.

- Our focus is the **time frame** between the entrance of Sin into the world until the Law came.

ADAM (Sin) ─────────────▶ THE LAW

Strong's first option (time frame) focuses on the what occurred during the period of time between the fall in the Garden and the Law of Moses (Genesis 3 to Exodus 34). This is where I believe the focus in the next statements is, so this is the definition we will use.

Even though the Law will be personified in the upcoming verses as a Ruler that helped Sin, Paul, in this flashback, is going to tell us important details about the condition of the world and the limits of Sin's power **before the Law entered the drama.**

...sin was in the world:

Sin was in the world before the law of Moses (2:1,12). It existed before the Law. We know this, because *"death passed upon all men, because all have sinned"* after Adam, and before the Law was given to Moses.

FACT: Continued personification of Sin, which is described as being in the **world, Sin is pictured as <u>outside of men</u> as a powerful conquering enemy—a powerful ruling entity** (cp. Gen. 4:7). I emphasize this, even though we know that *sins* are personal acts, because this is what Paul was inspired to write—we must follow the text. **Sin is used as a noun here.**

FACT: This statement, along with the next verse which states that Death was also in existence before the Law, prove Paul's point in the previous verse:

1. That Sin was in the world before the Law was given.

2. That **Death follows Sin**…and it all started with one man—Adam.

This is completely consistent with the apostle's pattern in the first 3 chapters of this letter: proving sin and guilt among the Heathen/Gentiles who incurred God's wrath (chp. 1), **before** introducing the sin and guilt of Jews who broke The Law given to them (chp. 2). **The heathen died because of sin and** without the Law! So, Sin and Death were in the world without the Law.

This is most likely the reason Paul's pattern is to elaborate on established and proven facts. (We must remember that Paul's readers where Gentiles who did not have the written Law to accuse them of sin. In fact, **the entire world** was condemned to darkness without a prophet or word from God from Noah and the flood until God chose and called Abram.)

Fact: Paul is proving his previous statement that Sin entered into the world *through* Adam, and Death *through* Sin **(neither came from the Law).**

Objection: Yes, **sin is lawlessness** (1John 3:4, KJV translates poorly. *Lit. Everyone who is doing the sin, the lawlessness also he doth do, and the sin is the lawlessness),* But, that is not **all t**hat sin is:

- It is failing to do good (Jam 4:17, the **omission** of a good deed);
- **Suppressing** innate truth given by God, resulting in God's wrath/anger (Rom. 1:19);
- It is **falsehood** (a lie), as opposed to truth (Rom. 3:4).

All of these conditions existed from Adam until Moses— *Sin was in the world.*

...but sin is not imputed when there is no law.

"But", is used here as an adverse conjunction, **introducing a contrary clause.** I does not mean "and", which would be introducing a cumulative and harmonious clause (adding one thing to another), instead of **subtracting** something.

But Sin is not:

The absolute negative. Sin is absolutely not...

imputed:

This is the first of only two uses of this controversial word in the New Testament: here and Philemon 1:18.

> Thayer's Definition: 1) to reckon in, set to one's account, lay to one's charge, impute

FACT: Sin is **absolutely not imputed** (charged to the account) under certain conditions—namely: **when there is no law**—during the period of time after Adam's sin and before Moses' Law!

This is a statement of absolute fact. There is no rational reason to believe that this verse is to be understood to mean the opposite of what it says.

Example of misinterpretation: "Adam broke the law of Moses in the garden". Some commentators actually teach this when interpreting this passage.

This verse clearly states that the law of Moses marked a definite point in history, and before that time Sin existed, but was not—could not—be imputed, because there was no law.

Now what does imputed mean? As we have seen, it is an accounting term which denotes marking a debt or credit to a ledger. However, in this passage it is a **legal accounting**, an official charge of debt/crime to a defendant's account.

Is the apostle saying in fact, that sin was not imputed (charged to account) before the Law of Moses? **If so (and it is so), how did the Law of Moses impute Sin when it came on the scene?**

Just so that we can understand this flashback better. If we glance back at 3:19-20 we can get a picture of exactly what effect the Law had on Sin by causing it to be imputed:

> Now we know that what things soever the law saith, it saith to them who are under the law: **that every mouth may be stopped,** and all the world **may become guilty** before God. Therefore by the deeds of the law there shall **no flesh be justified** in his sight: for by the law *is* **the knowledge of sin.**
> —Rom 3:19-20

Knowledge: *epignosis, recognition, full discernment, intimate knowledge.*

Through the Law's written rules of conduct, all men became aware of the crimes and transgressions they were committing, and the penalty for those crimes was death. So the law exposed and charged all of mankind's crimes and sins to their account...*for by the Law is the full knowledge of sin.*

If we see Sin as a noun in this passage: the Law pointed out Sin's powerful presence in the world, when before it was thought of as either weak or nonexistent.

The law **formally** (charged/registered trespass, and guilt), put mans sins on public record and personal conscious as a crime.[6] It ended all argument/debate; it presented a righteous standard that all agreed was punishable for disobedience—*ev-*

ery mouth attempting to claim self righteousness was stopped, and ll thw world became guilty before God.

All NT references to the Law's purpose and timing, declare its purpose and timing was to *register GUILT* on the conscious, as well as public record.

> Because the law worketh wrath: for **where no law is, there is no transgression.**
> —Rom 4:15

We see from the above verse which covers the same time period between Adam and the Law, that without the Law, there is no transgression. So, the Law puts down (imputes) violations as **transgressions** against its regulations. We'll go into more details in the next verse where Paul uses the word transgression.

FACT: To impute sin, does not mean *to punish* sin; And impute has no association with death: the penalty for transgression.

- You see, punishment has nothing to do with the law, punishment/death results from sin. *"The day you eat thereof you will surely die."*

- Death before the Law of Moses does not mean that sin was imputed, only that Sin existed; death results from **committing** sin. (A simple way of understanding this concept without leaving our drama, is to consider that when men err/sin from the path of life, they immediately experience death. It doesn't matter if a know that they have taken the wrong path as we will see.)

The confusion existing around the meaning of imputation in this verse, is simply due to ignoring its definition, and assuming it means the same thing as inflicting punishment.

FACT: The written Law and the resulting violations **prove** that the charge of sin, and it's penalty (Death,) are just and deserving. The Law shines a light on sin: gives true knowledge of it, and justifies death. It did this by defining the Law of God for men on planet earth. As we have seen all men agreed with its precepts to live by them.

> Now therefore, if ye will obey my voice indeed, and keep my covenant, then ye shall be a peculiar treasure unto me above all people: for all the earth is mine:..These are the words which thou shalt speak unto the children of Israel...**And all the people answered together, and said, All that the LORD hath spoken we will do.** And Moses returned the words of the people unto the LORD. —Exo 19:5 ff

> For when the Gentiles, which have not the law, do by nature the things contained in the law, these, having not the law, are a law unto themselves: Which shew the work of the law written in their hearts, their conscience also bearing witness... —Rom 2:14 -15

FACT: The text clearly says: sin is "absolutely not" charged to account, or put on public record, when there is no law. To suggest (as some do) that Paul means the opposite (there was a law before Moses) of what he explicitly says, is faulty interpretation.

In the same way: although we are chosen in Christ **before the foundation of the world** *(Eph 1:4, 1Cor. 1:30, Rom. 8:29 ff)*, making eternal life certain—righteousness **was not imputed** to believers **before the foundation of the world**, but, faith is put to our account as righteousness *when we believe in Christ,* **in our lifetime** (Rom. 3:22, 25.26; 4:3-5, 23, 25).

Faulty reasoning would say: since righteousness is imputed by faith, believers must be born with faith, since we were chosen in Christ before the foundation of the world. This reasoning ignores God's **timetable**. Justification/righteousness for the chosen is certain, but faith (in the lifetime) is necessary for its imputation (Rom. 8:28-30, 4:24). Likewise sin was real and active before Moses, but the Law was necessary for its imputation—to expose sin and stop every mouth. **Nowhere does the scripture say men's sins were imputed *in* Adam.**

Sin is not imputed where there is no law, and righteousness is not imputed where there is no faith.

Why is understanding Imputation Important?

Why did Paul take us back in time and point this out?

The Law offered to impute blessing or cursing, life or death, righteousness or sin, as a reward or penalty for obedience or violation—and it was official.

> Behold, I set before you this day a blessing and a curse; A blessing, if ye obey the commandments of the LORD your God, which I command you this day: And a curse, if ye will not obey the commandments of the

LORD your God, but turn aside out of the way which I command you this day, to go after other gods, which ye have not known.
—Deu. 11:26

Unfortunately, it was only able to impute sin, because all men committed the sin it forbade.

Objection!: Some (many Legalist, Pharisee's, Reformers, and Puritans—not all) believe the Law of Moses is *eternal,* and equal to, or greater than, New Covenant Grace. They suppose this verse teaches that there was the Law before Moses. They seriously err, like the Pharisees and other religious leaders at Galatia who stumbled at GRACE—essentially favoring Moses over Jesus. In this verse, The Law had a specific duration in time, when it entered the world—that was with Moses.

It is amazing how a entire system of theological doctrine regarding sin has been built upon the faulty interpretation of one verse; resting on a faulty definition of the word "impute" which appears only once in this epistle, and one other time in the whole NT. This serves to emphasize the importance of accepting the teachings of no man or system without careful personal examination of the facts. *(Acts 17:11)*

We know that **the law of Moses is not eternal**, because Christ is *"the end of the Law"* (Rom. 10), and against those who walk in the Spirt *"there is no law"* (Gal. 5)

The point of this verse is that Sin is not put down to the account of mankind when the written Law was not present.

Preview: We will learn that Sin used the promised blessings in the Law as enticement to gain Israel's agreement to the Covenant of Law, and thereby condemn them. (This will be discussed in the third book. Back to our present drama.)

Chapter Summary

> (For until the law sin was in the world: but sin is not imputed when there is no law.
> —Rom 5:13

- This second flashback introduces the third and last great conqueror of mankind into the drama—The Law.

- "For until the law" directs our attention to what occurred during the period of time between the fall and the Law of Moses (Genesis 3 to Exodus 34).

- *Sin was in the world* before the law of Moses (2:1,12). It existed before the Law. We know this, because *"death passed upon all men"* after Adam, and before the Law was given to Moses.

- Death has nothing to do with breaking law. It is not necessarily a legal punishment. It is a result of sin, or missing the mark, or falling short of God's glory. It passes to all sinners, whether they know they are sinners or not. When you *stray* from life you find death.

- The Law only brings the awareness of sin, So *"sin is not imputed"* or recorded on public record *"where there is no law."* So, Paul in Romans 7 could say, *"I would not have known that I lusted had not the Law said thou shall not lust"* In a sense, he was dying of cancer but didn't know why until the law identified the disease.

- Through its written code, all men became aware of the crimes they were committing, and the penalty for those crimes was listed as death So, the law charged all of mankind's crimes and sins to their account...*for by the Law is the knowledge of sin.*

- We are told in Romans 1, that although they didn't have the Law of Moses, they had innate knowledge given by God: *For God's wrath is revealed from Heaven on all ungodliness and unrighteousness of men, holding the truth in unrighteousness, because the thing known of God is clearly known within them, for God revealed it to them.* —Rom 1:18,19

- **Sin is not imputed where there is no law, and righteousness is not imputed where there is no faith.** Likewise faith is put down on our account as righteousness when we confess with our mouth our sin and that Jesus Christ is Lord. Rom. 4 & 10

- The Law simply proved that men are sinners. Before its entrance, Sin and Death were there, but not given their official legal descriptions and definitions.

- The Law is not eternal. In this verse, The Law had a specific duration in time, when it entered the world— that was with Moses.

- We know that **the law of Moses is not eternal**, because Christ is *"the end of the law" (Rom. 10), and* against those who walk in the Spirt *"there is no law" (Gal. 5)*

The Lawless Reign of Death

Third Major Observation in Flashback 2

*Sin may have needed the Law
to realize its full potential in the world,
but Death didn't!* —J. W.

Nevertheless death reigned from Adam to Moses, even over them that had not sinned, after the similitude of Adam's transgression, who is the figure of him that was to come. —**Rom. 5:14**

What this verse says:

This verse gives more details in the same flashback period discussed in the last verse: the period of time between Adam's sin and the Law of Moses (Genesis 3 to Exodus 34). The focus now is Death's reign as king:

What this verse DOESN'T Mean:

> John Gill commentary: Rom 5:14—Nevertheless death reigned from Adam to Moses...Though the law of Moses was not yet given, death exerted itself, and extended its dominion over all the sons and daughters of Adam, during the interval between Adam and Moses; which clearly shows that sin was in the world, *and that there must be a law in being, which that was a transgression of* (emphasis added): death is represented as a king, as sin and Satan sometimes are; and indeed, death reigns by sin, and Satan both by sin and death; their empires rise, stand, and fall together.

What this verse DOES mean:

Nevertheless:

This *transitional conjunction* introduces an exception, proving that Paul's intention in the previous verse was to show that there was no Law before Moses, otherwise "the exceptional condition" would not make sense. The exception (the nevertheless)—in my opinion—is not as Gill understood: To paraphrase Gill: *Even though the Law of Moses wasn't in existence, Death reigned through* **some other law.**

The *genuine* **"nevertheless" however, is:** *Despite* the Law of Moses not being in existence (to **pronounce** death as punishment for sin), Death still reigned over all of mankind. It reigned without the Law from Adam to Moses.

Now, *nevertheless* makes sense: because Death reigned without a law **pronouncing a penalty of condemnation and death, like God's command to Adam did.**

The written Law didn't add anything to Death's reign, it had all the power it needed to reign over sinners.

Why does Paul insert this exception?

Paul had to confirm his record of history, and the order of the entrance of the rulers of this world. He also had to correct any misunderstanding about the relationship between Sin, Death, and the Law. So, he inserts this "nevertheless" to highlight The Law's absence during that period of time between Adam and Moses. Let's not make the mistake he is trying to prevent by adding some law in that time-frame.

THE THREE DEADLY ALLIES

To help us appreciate the Law's importance, let's switch scenes to Paul's letter to Corinth for another perspective:

> The sting [poison] of death *is* sin; and the strength [power] of sin *is* the law. —1Cor. **15:56**

The poison that causes Death is Sin, and the strength of that poison is the Law. The Law increased the potency of Sin. In real life, **it broadened Sin's territory** by reaching into the heart/motives as well as the actions of mankind—"love God with all your <u>heart, mind, and strength</u>, and your neighbor as yourself." Or, from a medical perspective: it made men sicker, by pointing out all areas of disease, like a cancer diagnosis. **Thereby, the Law became a powerful friend to Sin's reign.**

So then, looking back from the beginning: Sin was in the world from Adam to Moses, but it was not imputed, because The Law was non-existent. *Nevertheless,* during the same period Death reigned as devastating King over everyone!

Paraphrase: Despite there not being the Law, or the imputation of sin... Death reigned as dictatorial King from Adam to Moses—even over them that had not **sinned** equivalent to Adam's transgression.

We err (along with Gill, *pg. 63*) if we suppose that Paul's point in v.14 is to show that "**Sin was in the world** between Adam and Moses": He already established that fact in the previous two verses:

> Wherefore, as by one man sin entered into the world, and death by sin; and so death passed upon all men, for that all have sinned: (For until the law [Sin] was in the world: but [Sin] is not imputed when there is no law...)—**Rom. 5:12**

Also, as far as Paul **implying** that there *"being a law during that period of time"* as Gill and others teach: Paul clearly states in the previous verse that the period of time between Adam and the Law of Moses was marked by "NO LAW". *(For until the law sin was in the world: but sin is not imputed when there is no law. —Rom 5:13)*

To teach that Paul meant the very opposite of what he said is serious error, and faulty exposition, or adding to the text of scripture in an attempt to prove one's own ideas, or carelessly passing on erroneous teaching without independently investigating the facts. Preachers and teachers have to be very careful not to poison the truth! (See appendix "A Law Before Moses", for an explanation of what some have to gain from this error)

Paul is personifying Death as a king, so that Christ's conquest and dominion will be magnified by comparison. Paul is defending his assertion that we will be saved by Christ's *life,* by flashing back to the devastating reign of *Death* over the entire human race...

even over them *[obviously comparing these people with Adam]* **that had not sinned after...**

John Gill in his commentary (*pg. 63*) makes the mistake of viewing the picture presented in this passage and immediately focusing on **what it doesn't say**, as opposed to focusing on what it does say[8]. Remember, rule #1 of Bible interpretation is: **what does the text say**!

He makes the assumption that when Paul says *"even over them that had not sinned after the likeness of Adam's sin"*, Paul is <u>implying</u> there is a class of people **who did sin in the manner** Adam did—in this text there are NO SUCH PEOPLE.

(I don't mean to confuse you here, but Gill is not the only one to interpret this verse that way—it's a very common interpretation—I'm not picking on him, he's one of my favorites.)

Nevertheless, this is what we call "reading between the lines".

It appears to me, that the word "even" stresses a noteworthy **distinction:** Death reigned as dictatorial King over two classes of people: Adam, and those who did not commit sin in the manner he did. *This is "even" a marvel, because Death destroyed them all equally.*

Paul has already said that Sin entered the world through Adam: We know that Adam died because he was **disobedient** to God's prohibition not to eat from *"the tree of the knowledge of good and evil."*

Death passed upon all men because they too sinned. They sinned **without a direct prohibition,** because before Moses there was no oral or written Law from God.

Definitions of the Greek word for sinned:

Note that transgressing the Law is only one definition! This is consistent with the Bibles use of the word **hamartia (sin):**

Thayer Definition:

1a) to be without a share in

1b) to miss the mark

1c) to err, be mistaken

1d) to miss or wander from the path of uprightness and honor, to do or go wrong...

Hamartia usually refers to erring from the perfect standard, it is broader than other words which refer to breaking some spoken or written command. If we think of **"certain** sins" when we see this word in The New Testament, we may miss its true intent of pointing out **our condition** in relation to God's purpose when he made us. Whenever we come up short of that standard we are a sinner—we have erred.

So, *"even over them that had not sinned after the similitude of Adams transgression"* is not new information. It is simply a deeper explanation of what has already been said. It draws a distinction between Adam's sin and everyone else's.

Chapters 1-2 does the same thing when it distinguishes between the wrath incurring sins of the Gentiles, who only had God given innate revelation, and the Jews who had the prohibitions of the Law of Moses. So, God's wrath and judgment hangs, *even* over them (Gentiles) that had not **sinned** after the similitude of the Jews *transgression*—they had no direct commands/laws—the Jews did.

...after the Similitude

> Thayer: that which has been made after the likeness of something. 1b) likeness, i.e. resemblance, such as amounts almost to equality or identity.

Note: Clearly they did not commit anything **similar to** Adam's sin: This statement *destroys* the idea of sin imputed to all men *in* Adam, because, if they sinned "in Adam" that would be the ***very exact*** similitude of Adams sin—think about this!

...of Adam's transgression...

The use of the different words: ***sinned*** and ***transgression*** is noteworthy and intentional.

Thayer's definition of transgressed: 2b) the breach of a definite, promulgated, ratified law

Although similar, the words have a different *emphasis*. They *missed the mark*, but Adam *transgressed*: Adam disobeyed a direct command/prohibition, those without the Law erred from innate knowledge of the truth (Rom. 1:18); **Death reigned king over them all.**

> Rom 2:23 Thou that makest thy boast of the law, through **breaking** *[transgressing]* the law dishonourest thou God?

The above verse is the first of three uses of the word transgress in this letter. This verse is spoken to Jews who received the Law and broke its commands.

> Rom 4:15 Because the law worketh wrath: for where no law is, there is no **transgression.**

This is the second time Paul used the word. We mentioned it in the last chapter under imputation, that the Law is necessary to impute sin. When there is no Law there can be no transgression, because transgression refers to the sin of breaking a known law. In the verse above, "the law works wrath" because it charge sin to the account of the guilty violator as a crime deserving punishment or death.

Adam **transgressed** the command given to him from God, the others, referred to here in verse 14, **erred**—Death reigned over them all.

To use the analogy of poison again:

> The sting [poison] of death *is* sin; and the strength [power] of sin *is* the law. —1Cor. 15:56

Death reigned even over those who didn't drink a powerful Law injected dose of Sin. Their sin was less potent, Adam's was straight!

This verse shows that all sin is deadly, even though there are degrees of potency. (cp. Matt. 10:15, Jam. 3:1)

> Verily I say unto you, It shall be more tolerable for the land of Sodom and Gomorrha in the day of judgment, than for that city.

> My brethren, be not many masters, knowing that we shall receive the greater condemnation.

FACT: With that in mind, it is safe to say, all of the sins of the Gentiles in Rom. 1:18-31 were **not** committed *"after the similitude of Adams transgression."* (Again the context teaches!)

INFANTS?

FACT: Paul, earlier in this letter stated:

> What then? are we better than they? No, in no wise: for we have before proved both Jews and Gentiles, that they are all under sin; As it is written, There is none righteous, no, not one: —**Rom 3:9**

Proving by facts, **all men** (no exceptions given—not even infants) are guilty sinners deserving God's wrath, and Death.

The Law came along and confirmed this:

> Now we know that what things soever the law saith, it saith to them who are under the law: that *every* mouth may be stopped, and **all** the world may become guilty before God. —**Rom 3:19**

There is no reason to assume that *"every mouth may be stopped and **all** the world may become guilty before God"* doesn't include infants. *Every* and *all* are the same word in the Greek original, it means the whole. In this case the whole world of mankind.

FACT: Paul doesn't mention infants specifically because they are included in his previous statements: "death passed upon **all** men because **all** have sinned (erred)"

FACT: The only exception Paul mentions here is a class of people who didn't sin in the exact way that Adam did, yet Death reigned over them also. This group did sin, it was just not like Adam's sin.

The unique thing about Adam's sin, is that it was disobedience to a direct command from God, i.e. "do not eat". Whereas every other human being between Adam and Moses sinned by *"falling short of His glory"* (**God's perfect design for mankind made in His image.**) *Rom:3:23*

FACT: Everyone who dies is a sinner and has sinned. (Rom 6:23 For the wages of sin is death;) The propensity to err (imperfection) is inherent by nature in the fabric of all of Adam's offspring. *(Psa 51:5 Behold, I was shapen in iniquity; and in sin did my mother conceive me.)* cp. Gen 8:21. Rom 7:18, *For I know that in me (that is, in my flesh), dwelleth no good thing: Rom.3:10ff*

FACT: There are **no innocent** souls according to the Bible, and our conduct proves this is true. Sin is the very seed of opposition to, and deviation from GOD's glory (perfect intent to glorify Him as image barrier). Anyone born who is not what God intended Adam to be when he created him is a sinner—they have *missed the mark, and fall short of God's glory.*

One other fact about "innocent infants": Adam and Eve's offspring are said to be *created after their likeness,* which includes the sentence of death resulting from sin.

Finally: many of those who argue that infants are suggested in this passage *(see Endnote 8),* as having Adam's sin imputed to them (through seminal headship), also teach that "had not sinned in the similitude" refers to infants.—**this is a very serious contradiction.** If all mankind sinned "in Adam" then there are no innocent infants, because they also sinned the exact sin in the garden. For more arguments on this topic see Index[9].

Romans 3 is very important in any discussion on the sins and guilt of mankind which result in God's wrath, judgement and death. Because Paul uses the Psalms, not the ten commandments to prove humanity's guilt! And the focus is on the heart, mind, thoughts, desires, speech etc. (Sin's territory expanded!)

> As it is written, There is none righteous, no, not one: There is none that understandeth, there is none that seeketh after God. They are all gone out of the way, they are together become unprofitable; there is none that doeth good, no, not one. Their throat *is*

an open sepulchre; with their tongues they have used deceit; the poison of asps *is* under their lips: Whose mouth *is* full of cursing and bitterness: Their feet *are* swift to shed blood: Destruction and misery *are* in their ways: And the way of peace have they not known: There is no fear of God before their eyes. Now we know that what things soever the law saith, it saith to them who are under the law: that every mouth may be stopped, and all the world may become guilty before God. —**Rom 3:10-19**

So, we see that Paul has already proved Death's reign over "those who did not sin after the similitude of Adam's transgression."

Paul's main point is not to highlight different types of sin, but to highlight the vast and devastating reign of Death in the cosmos, because of Sin, but without the Law.

Chapter Summary

Nevertheless death reigned from Adam to Moses, even over them that had not sinned, after the similitude of Adam's transgression, who is the figure of him that was to come. —**Rom. 5:14**

- This statement gives more details of the same flashback period discussed in the last verse: the period of time between Adam's sin and the Law of Moses, emphasizing **Death's reign.**

- *Nevertheless:* indicates Death reigned without any law **pronouncing a penalty of condemnation and death,** like God's command to Adam in the garden did.
- The highlight of this flashback is: The Law ***didn't add*** anything to **Death's reign**, it had all the devastating power it needed.
- "even over them" stresses an noteworthy **distinction: Between Adam and everyone else,** Death reigned as dictatorial King over two classes of people: Adam and those who did not commit sin in the manner he did—and it is "even" a marvel, because Death destroyed both classes of people equally—the one that had a command and those without a law.
- This verse shows that all sin is deadly; Even though there are degrees of potency! Adam ***"transgressed"*** a law; everyone else ***"erred"*** (sinned) from God's design.
- Death results from sin of any kind, wether known or not. **Everyone who dies is a sinner and has sinned.** (Rom 6:23, *For the wages of sin is death;*)
- There are **no innocent** souls according to the Bible, and our conduct proves this is true. Sin is the very seed of opposition to, and deviation from GOD's glory (perfect intent to glorify Him as his image barrier). Anyone born who is not what God intended Adam to be when he created him is a sinner—they have *missed the mark, and fall short of God's glory.*
- All of the information in this flashback was proven in chapters 1-3 of Romans—it's not new information.

The Foreshadowing: Figure

Fifth Major Observation in Flashback 2

...who is the figure of him that was to come.

N ow, through this flashback, Paul reveals **new information** for the first time in this letter. He's about to reveal why he flashed back to Adam in the first place.

We must remind ourselves that Paul's main purpose is to persuade us that "we joy in God through our Lord Jesus Christ, through whom we have received the atonement." So, he now tells us, the one who caused us to be in need of atonement in the first place is a type of the One who was to come and rescue us. Since he is a type of Christ, we will learn something from Him.

The reign of Death happened because of Adam's unique transgression; and he was a **type** of Jesus Christ who would come after him and end Death's reign.

Definition: A figure or type is something that **resembles** something else; like a statue, or the image on money. It can also mean a **sample** of something like a **model** plane, or an architectural model of a building. However, the figure **represents** something—it's **not equal** to the thing, it simply resembles it.

In the Old Testament there were many figures/types of Christ, which *pre*figured/foreshadowed various aspects of his person or work. This is true, because the story of human history is essentially the history of redeeming the fallen and hostile race; and Jesus Christ is the **sole means** of accomplishing that reconciliation—therefore he is pictured in *every single piece* of that puzzle relating to redemption. The first promise of salvation in the Bible refers to Jesus as the seed:

> And I will put enmity between thee and the woman, and between thy seed and her seed; it shall bruise thy head, and thou shalt bruise his heel. —Gen 3:15

He is typified in the animal that was killed to provide clothing for Adam and Eve in the garden (Gen. 3:21).

Therefore, it stands to reason that every means of accomplishing the salvation of men would come through him from that time forward.

> And beginning at Moses and all the prophets, he expounded unto them in all the scriptures the things concerning himself.
> —Luk 24:27

As an important side-note: the fact that the type is **not equal to the person or thing it represents** is the reason why Paul was led by God to reprimand the Colossians, Galatians, and the Hebrews for clinging to Old Testament types after Christ had already come.

> Let no man therefore judge you in meat, or in drink, or in respect of an holy day, or of the new moon, or of the sabbath *days:* Which are a shadow of things to come; but the body *is* of Christ. —Col 2:16

In the above passage, the figure is described as the shadow cast, (like the sun), by Christ's physical body. They were shadows from the heavenly person. But, now that the real person has come, we no longer need to marvel at his shadow. The Colossians were—in essence—clinging to a shadow on the ground, instead of the person of Jesus Christ. The figure or type merely represents the person, **without any spiritual or earthly power of its own—it is temporary.** In the NT, it is clear that **every single type was replaced** by the appearance of Jesus Christ himself.

> For the law having a shadow of good things to come, and not the very image of the things, can never with those sacrifices which they offered year by year continually make the comers thereunto perfect He

taketh away the first, that he may establish the second. —Heb 10:1

On the other hand, before we misunderstand this comparison, and get carried away with this typography, Paul will tell us next, exactly what he means, **and what he doesn't mean by the word "figure".**

This is the end of Flashback 2, but now we have much improved sight, knowledge, and understanding.

Chapter Summary

> ...who is the figure of him that was to come.
> —Rom. 5:14

- Paul reveals **new information** for the first time in this letter. He reveals why he flashed back to Adam in the first place.

- He now tells us, the one who got us in this mess in the first place (Adam) is a type the One who was to come and rescue us. Since Adam is a type of Christ, we will learn something from Him.

- A figure or type is something that **resembles** something else, like a statue, or the image on money. It can also mean a **sample** of something like a **model** plane, or an architectural model of a building. However, the figure **represents** something—it's **not equal** to the thing, it simply resembles it.

- The story of human history is one of redeeming the fallen and hostile race; and Jesus Christ is the **sole means** of accomplishing that reconciliation—hence, he is pictured in *every single piece* of that puzzle relating to redemption. The first promise of salvation in the Bible refers to Jesus as the seed of the women who would crush the serpent's head.

- The fact that the type is **not equal to the person or thing it represents,** is the reason why Paul was led by God to reprimand the Colossians, Galatians, and the Hebrews, for clinging to Old Testament types after Christ had already come in person.
- This leads to the next highlights...

A Type of Contrast

Now, back to our MAIN SCENE

> *And I wept much, because no man was found worthy to open and to read the book, neither to look thereon. And one of the elders saith unto me, Weep not: behold, the Lion of the tribe of Judah, the Root of David, has prevailed to open the book, and to loose the seven seals thereof.*
> —*Rev 5:4*

This portion of the drama returns to the main scene, in verse 12, which reads "Wherefore as"; We will flash back and forth between Adam and Jesus comparing their influence on the world.

A common error in Bible study is to ignore the details of passages which appear to be redundant or repetitious. The truth is: these passages don't just repeat the same information in different ways; they view the same scene from different angles, so that we understand the truth more fully. Think of it as different camera angles of the same scene. This method makes it less likely for misunderstanding, and provides a fuller understanding of the truth presented.

The end result of viewing this present drama from many different angles is: any way you look at it Jesus is much greater than Adam, and all the enemies he let into the cosmos!

King Death Conquered by the Grace of God and the Gift

<u>But not as the offence, so also is the free gift.</u> (For if through the offence of one many be dead, **much more** the grace of God, and the gift by grace, which is **by** one man, Jesus Christ, hath abounded unto many.) *16. And **not** as it was by one that sinned, so is the gift: for the judgment was by one to condemnation, **but the free gift** is of many offences unto justification.* (**17.** For if by one man's offence **death reigned** by one; **much more** they which receive abundance of grace and of the gift of righteousness **shall reign in life by one**, Jesus Christ.) *18. Therefore as by **the offence of one** judgment came upon all men to **condemnation;** even so by **the righteousness of one** the free gift came upon all men unto justification of life.* **19.** For as by one man's disobedience many were made sinners, so by the obedi-

> ence of one shall many be made righteous.
> —Rom 5:15-18

Structure of The Proof Section

This passage is very difficult to understand without recognizing the following structure:

1) In verse 15, Paul tells us right away that the typology between Adam and Jesus is a contrast between Adams sin and Jesus' "free gift". **This is the conclusion, thesis, or truth, he will prove in the next 3 verses (16,17,18).**

    a) In verse 19, after proving that the two figures are different, and Jesus is greater than Adam, Paul restates this conclusion as absolute proven fact!: *Rom. 5:15, 19* **But <u>not</u>** *as the offence, so also is the free gift... For as by one man's disobedience many were made sinners, so by the obedience of one shall many be made righteous.*

    The "offense" in v. 15 is explained as the "disobedience" in v. 19; And the "free gift" as "righteousness"

2) Just as verse 15 states the fact, and v. 19 explains that fact, Paul proves his main point by stating two facts, then evidence to support those facts. (The difficulty in understanding this passage is because of his structure or style of argument—but the Holy Spirit is guiding him.)

3) Paul doesn't state a fact then immediately explain it before moving on to the next fact—which would seem more logical. The two facts are presented first;

then the first one is explained, followed by the second:

    a) The 1st. fact proving the contrast between Jesus and Adam, and its explanation are in V. 15b & 17: Through Adam's offense **Death reigned**; through Jesus' gift of righteousness **Life reigns.**

    b) The 2nd. fact/proof, and its explanation are in V. 16 & 18: Through Adam, judgment resulting in **condemnation** came upon all men; through Jesus, **justification** resulting in life came upon all men.

4) Next, we have the conclusion we've already discussed (15a & 19), followed by the "moreover" (or "but wait there's even more"), added to Christ's greatness in the last two verses.

Simple Structure: 15a (argument)→**15b-18** (proof)→**19** (conclusion)

(When they insist the Bible is simple, don't believe them:-)

So, now that we know the logic of the structure of Paul's (Spirit inspired) argument, let's get into the details.

*15a **But not** [absolute negative] **as the offense, so also is the free gift...19. For as by one man's disobedience many were made sinners, so by the*** obedience of one shall many be made righteous.

Although we know the conclusion of this flashback to Adam, and it's connection to verse 15. Let's wait (as Paul did) to examine the details of verse 19—there are some real gems of truth there. For now the first half:

15a Lit. *But the free gift/righteousness is not also like the disobedience.*

> **RWP:** It is more contrast than parallel: "the trespass" (the slip, fall to one side) over against the free gift.

This is EXTREMELY important!:

The Purpose of vv. 15-19 is obviously to explain the last phrase: *"who is the figure of him that was to come."*

So, Paul begins immediately to prevent the very error that currently exists among many Bible teachers, by defining what he does and does not mean by "figure/type".

Paul begins with an ***absolute negative statement: "but not as";*** emphasizing that the type (figure) is more contrast than harmony. **He is saying that (in significant ways), Adam is opposite of Jesus—not identical!**

The "type" therefore refers to their individual influence on the entire human race (many/all) for death or life. **But the typology is by no means exact and parallel** as many commentators insist. So, *"the free gift is absolutely not like the* *offense"* begins the comparison between Adam and Jesus, the type and anti-type.

We have seen from the comparison between the opening and closing statements, that "the **offence**" was "**disobedience**".

...15a But not as the offense, so also is the free gift...19. For as by <u>one</u> man's disobedience <u>many</u> were made sinners, so by the obedience of <u>one</u> shall <u>many</u> be made righteous.

As Paul goes on to explain what he means by *Adam is a type of Jesus Christ, and the offense is not like the gift...*

1. The first thing we will notice is the repetition of the number "***One***", used as a pronoun for both Adam and Jesus. This word is used **12 times in 10 verses.** It is therefore a key to understanding what the type refers to: **One** single man caused sin and death, **one** single man is responsible for righteousness and life.

2. The next thing we notice is the repetition of the word "***many***"; It is used 7 times in 7 verses, starting at our current verse. By the way, the adjective "all" occurs only 4 times in 2 verses, so the support for "every single human being saved through Jesus" is weak. The all refers to the many—all (every one, the whole group) of the many.

Before we look at how Paul uses these words to teach us important truths about how Adam is a type of Jesus, we must remember, the idea of one affecting many is not new.

He introduces this flashback to explain the earlier declaration about Jesus:

> ...**Much more** then, being now justified by his blood, *we* [many, all] shall be saved from wrath **through him**. For if, when *we* [many, all] were enemies, *we* [many, all] were reconciled to God by the death of his Son, much more, being reconciled, *we* [many, all] shall be saved by **his life**. And not only *so*, but *we* [many, all] also joy in God through our Lord Jesus Christ, **by whom** *we* [many, all] have now received the atonement. —**Rom 5:9-11**

As you will have noticed, we have the very same phrase "**much more**", used in verse 9 as assurance that *we* (many, all of us) will be saved through Jesus Christ.

In fact, this "one affecting many" idea actually began in verse one.:

> Therefore being justified by faith, *we* [many, all] have peace with God through our Lord Jesus Christ: —Rom. 5:1

So, Paul will now *cement, in the minds of his readers,* the fact that ONE MAN can provide salvation for all who believe in him among the entire human race, as the gospel promises.

Chapter Summary

> But not as *[absolutely not as]* the offence, so also is the free gift...—**Rom. 5:15**

- This portion of the drama returns to the main scene, in verse 12 which said "Wherefore as"; It will flash back and forth between Adam and Jesus comparing their influence on the world.
- We are told that the "as" comparing Jesus with Adam is not a complementary comparison, but mostly a contrast.
- Think of the repetition as different camera angles of the same scene. So, repetition and redundancy are very important teaching tools in the Bible.
- The difficult structure is as follows: Verse 15 is the thesis which verses 16-18 will prove. In verse 19, after proving that the two figures are different, and Jesus is greater than Adam, Paul will restate his thesis as absolute proven fact!: *Rom. 5:15, 19* **But not <u>as</u> the offence, so also is the free gift... For <u>as</u> by one man's disobedience many were made sinners, so by the obedience of one shall many be made righteous.*
- The "offense" in v. 15 (our current focus), is explained as the "disobedience" in v. 19; And the "free gift" in v. 15, is "righteousness in v. 19" Disobedience made many sinners, obedience gave many the (unearned) free gift of righteousness.
- Paul is now about to offer the proof, through historical facts, that the one man Jesus can provide all of the blessings talked about starting at verse 1, to **all, many, the whole group, who have faith** in him.

Proof 1: The Gift is Not Like the Offense

The One who gave Life is Greater than the One who caused Death

> *I am the door: by me if any man enter in, he shall be saved, and shall go in and out, and find pasture. The thief cometh not, but for to steal, and to kill, and to destroy: I am come that they might have **life**, and that they might have it more abundantly.* — Joh. 10:9

> But not as the offence, so also is the free gift. **(For if through the offence of one many be dead, much more the grace of God, and the gift by grace, which is by one man, Jesus Christ, hath abounded unto many.)** — Rom. 5:15

...15b For if through the offence of one many be dead...

Verses 15b & 17: Through Adam's offense, Death reigned over the human race.

After stating emphatically that the comparison between Adam and Jesus is a contrast, this is his **first proof** that the free gift of the one man Jesus, is not like the offense of the one man Adam. This comparison is between death and life. He is restating and proving v. 12. "*Wherefore, as by one man sin entered into the world, and death by sin; and so death passed upon all men, for that all have sinned:*"

much more the grace of God, and the gift by grace...

"Much more the grace of God..."; *To a surpassing greater degree*, because, Death had conquered all men; Therefore, the rescue (grace) has to be **much greater**. **Grace** is receiving blessing from God when we deserve punishment. Paul is establishing his initial point about salvation through Jesus. (also compare chp. 4:2-5):

> ...And hope maketh not ashamed; because the love of God is shed abroad in our hearts

by the Holy Ghost which is **given** *[grace in action]* unto us. For when we were yet **without strength**, in due time Christ died **for the ungodly**. For scarcely for a righteous man will one die: yet peradventure for a good man some would even dare to die. But God commendeth his love toward us, in that, **while we were yet sinners**, Christ died for us. **Much more** then, being now justified by his blood, we shall be saved from wrath through him. For if, when we were enemies, we were reconciled to God by the death of his Son, **much more**, being reconciled, we shall be saved by his life… —Rom 5:5-10

"I am come that they might have **life**, and that they might have it **more abundantly** *[much more]*."

Can you see the importance of remembering the context as you interpret the passage?

"Much more the grace of God and [even] **The Gift**": means receiving something at no cost to you. **In this letter it also describes something we could never afford—the price is greater than our means to pay—abundant riches given to the impoverished!** As we shall see in verse 17, the grace and gift is *righteousness (to rebellious sinners who believe)*.

This is not new theology either, Paul has already established these truths:

> For **all** have sinned, and come short of the glory of God; Being **justified freely** *[the gift of righteousness]* by [dia] his **grace** through

the redemption that is in Christ Jesus:...—
Rom 3:23-26

As you can see, Paul's earlier statement about *the gift of righteousness and grace* is repeated and elaborated upon here in a different context—showing just how important it is. Chapter 3 introduced the free gift as fact, chapter 5 is showing the power it took to accomplish it. Notice how doctrine is built upon itself in teaching.

...which is by one man, Jesus Christ, hath abounded unto many.

The One affected many. As we pointed out earlier, the purpose is to establish beyond a doubt, that the one man Jesus Christ can reconcile us to God, and save us from the wrath of God which is to come *(5:10);* Therefore, the repetition of *one* and *many*. The grace and gift have One source—Jesus Christ. (By the way, this truth excludes all other ways to heaven!)

hath Abounded, is equal to my idea of *Overkill*. It means to excel or super abound—over-kill gives the correct sense of **even greater force over the offense and Death**—it is excessive force. This word will be used again at the end of chapter five to summarize the whole teaching!

Compare: "*I am come that they might have* **life***, and that they might have* it **more abundantly**."

> **Lit. trans.:** *But the free gift is not also like the deviation. For if by the deviation of the one the many died, much more the grace of*

God, and the gift in grace, which is of the one Man, Jesus Christ, did abound to the many.

Now we skip verse 16 to get the fuller explanation of the point Paul just made. He will shed more light on "many be **dead**" and "the gift of grace hath...**abounded** unto many". Remember v15b is the fact/proof and v17 is the explanation. (See pg 83)

v.17 For if by one man's offense death reigned [to rule as king] **by one; much more** [to a greater degree] **they which receive** [to take] **abundance** [superabundantly, superiority, preeminence] **of grace and of the gift of righteousness shall reign in life by one, Jesus Christ.**

Lit: *For if by the deviation of the one, Death reigned through the one, much more those who are taking hold of the super abundance of grace and the gift of righteousness shall rule in life through the One: Jesus Christ.*

(We must stop to appreciate the power of the verse we just read! This may very well be one of the greatest gospel verses in the New Testament. Let's see why.)

One man's offense/deviation...
The offense is the disobedience of Adam in the garden.

...death reigned
Another **personification of Death** as ruler, for the purpose of emphasizing its dominance over the human race, and exalting the greater ruler/conqueror—Life, through Jesus Christ.

Laying Hold of the Power of God!

Verse 17 gets to the title of our book: It highlights a striking transfer of POWER: Death reigned as king over all of humanity, yet its reign was supplanted, over-ruled by more powerful kings—*US*. **We who receive super abundance of grace and the gift of righteousness.**

Paul told us in 1:16: *"the gospel of Christ...is the power [force] of God unto salvation to everyone that believeth"*. **Now, he gives proof of this power in profound action!**

Although Death reigned King,; **to a much greater degree** *those who take...* (This is no doubt an increase in power through acquisition.) The power it took for Death to secure its throne over mankind was exceeded—surpassed!

The word translated **"they which receive",** literally means *"to take to one's self, to make one's own"*. It definitely refers to the many exhortations to **believe (exercise faith)** in this letter up to this point (Cp.3:22,26,28, 4:5,12,16,24), particularly:

> ...I am not ashamed of the gospel of Christ: for it is **the power of God** unto salvation to **every one that believeth**...The just shall **live by faith**. —Rom 1:16

So, "they which take possession of abundance of grace" are the same as *those who grasp the power of God (the gospel) by faith*. In the above verse, this power is given "to" believers, in 5:17 the emphasis is on the faith that grasps that power.

Paul is not ashamed, because in this war he knows he has been given the Atomic Bomb that will destroy the enemies and deliver the captives.

This verse doesn't support the "federal headship" of Adam and Jesus, because the comparison is Death reigning through Adam, but *the many* reigning (not because of imputation *in* Christ), but by **taking hold** of God's power.! **Therefore, righteousness is not a passively received gift—on the contrary—it is taken or laid hold of through faith!** *The gift is grasped!*

What Exactly is FAITH?

This question is so very important we will need to take a recess from our drama to sit down and get a clear picture of this important concept.

Looking at the verse above, notice that **Faith is not the power**—it is the hand that gasps the power of God inside the gospel, believing/faithing is the disposition of those who hold on to that power. (Compare Mat. 8:10, 15:28, even great faith grasps God's power.)

Faith is an act of obedience to the Gospel's call for repentance

...through whom we did receive grace and apostleship, for obedience of faith among all the nations, in behalf of his name; among whom are also ye, the called of Jesus Christ; —Rom 1:5

Faith is an action verb, it begins, and continues throughout the life. It is the opposite of ungodliness

For the righteousness of God in it [the gospel] is revealed from faith to faith, according as it hath been written, 'And the righteous one by faith shall live,' for revealed is the wrath of God from heaven upon all ungodliness and unrighteousness of men, who hold down the truth in unrighteousness. —Rom 1:17

Faith is confidence in God or Jesus's word

Rom 3:26 To declare, I say, at this time his righteousness: that he might be just, and the justifier of him which believeth in Jesus.

In the verse above, faith is believing in Jesus's word *"who ever believes in me has everlasting life, I am the way, the truth, the life...ect."* Faith is not believing that anything you wish for you will get because you have "faith". The power is in the One I believe in to deliver on his word—in this case: Jesus's power to make me righteous before God and save me.

Faith is a LAW greater than the law of Moses

> Rom 3:27 Where is boasting then? It is excluded. By what law? of works? Nay: but by **the law of faith**. Therefore **we conclude** that a man is justified by faith without the deeds of the law

Faith is the Law which justifies men whom the Law of Works condemned. It is distinct and separate from the law of works.

Faith is NOT A WORK, it's the opposite of work

> Now to him that worketh is the reward not reckoned of grace, but of debt. But to him that worketh not, but believeth on him that justifieth the ungodly, his faith is counted for righteousness. —Rom 4:4

These verses teach that faith is not a work or effort that creates a credit with God, so now he has to pay you what you've earned. You've given him faith and he owes you eternal life. Or you've done the required work and obligated him to pay you.

No, you need faith to believe that God can "justify a godly" person like yourself. Because you believe that God can justify ungodly people who believe that he can save this way, He "counts/credits to your account (imputes) righteousness."

Why is faith so important to God? Because no man possesses it of himself, we are by nature unbelievers, remember: *Rom 3:10 As it is written, There is none righteous,* **no, not one:** *There is* **none** *that understandeth, there is none that seeketh after God.*

HOW DO WE KNOW THAT FAITH IS A GRIFT FROM GOD AND NOT OUR OWN GOOD WORK?

When God called us to believe in Christ we were spiritually dead, enemies against him, sinners:

> And hope maketh not ashamed; because the love of God is shed abroad in our hearts by the Holy Spirit which is given unto us. For when **we were yet without strength**, in due time Christ died for the **ungodly**. For scarcely for a righteous man will one die: yet peradventure for a good man some would even dare to die. But God commendeth his love toward us, in that, while **we were yet sinners**, Christ died for us. —Rom 5:5

So, "they which take possession of abundance of grace" are the same as *those who grasp the power of God (the gospel) by faith.*

THROUGH FAITH WE RECEIVE THE RIGHTEOUSNESS REQUIRED FOR ENTRANCE INTO THIS STATE OF GRACE

> Rom 5:1 Therefore being justified by faith, we have peace with God through our Lord Jesus Christ: By whom also we have access by faith into this grace wherein we stand, and rejoice in hope of the glory of God.

<u>**Faith is a verb not an noun.**</u> **And, it is more powerful than Death; faith is the hand that clinches the power of God and takes hold of...**

...abundance [superabundant, superior, preeminence] **of grace** [lovingkindness, favor] **and of the gift of righteousness**

The Powers which free the captives from the devastating reign of Death are SUPER, SUPERIOR, PREEMINENT! They are Faith, Grace, and the gift of Righteousness. The word "and" usually means "even". So, The abundance of grace is the gift of righteousness to undeserving sinners who believe.

Righteousness is always described as "the gift," because it is not *self righteousness* (a product of our own work), which Paul has proven. It is through belief in someone else's work/righteousness.

> Rom 1:16 For I am not ashamed of the gospel of Christ: **for it is the power of God unto salvation** to every one that believeth; to the Jew first, and also to the Greek. **For therein is the righteousness of God revealed from faith to faith:** as it is written, The just shall live by faith. —Rom 1:16, 17

When we remember verse 17 in the first chapter, we are able to get an even clearer picture of this abundant grace. The gift we take hold of, is the righteousness inside the gospel in the above verse. It is the ***gunpowder***—so to speak—inside of the gospel which gives it devastating power. In 5:17 this power is taken hold of; and in 1:17 we were told that this power is given **to** those who live by faith.

So, now we know why Paul, in the face of all enemies, was not the least bit humiliated, embarrassed, or ashamed of the gospel. Because it is the superabundant power of the gracious God to enable the FAITH possessing Saints to...

...reign in life

Reign in life, in contrast to being under the dominion of Death's reign. Life is not only the coveted treasure of those who are seeking freedom from slavery under Sin and Death, but it is the single most valuable treasure for everyone who lives on planet earth. It is, for those subject to Death's dominion, a destination—"reign **in the realm** of life". To possess this life in surpassing abundance, overflowing, is beyond anything we could ask for, imagine, or comprehend this side of heaven! Yet, it is for this very reason Jesus came to earth.

"*I am come that they might have* **life**, *and that they might have it* **more abundantly**."—*John 10:10*

And some helpful preacher told you that "life more abundantly" referred to earthly riches? "Might have life" means there was none before he came. "More abundantly" suggests a potential to "superabound". Now we know what Jesus meant!

We must compare this blessed state with the state of grace Paul opens this chapter with. All of the same elements are there: faith, grace, righteousness/justification, realm of life:

> Rom 5:1 Therefore being justified by faith, we have peace with God through our Lord Jesus Christ: By whom also we have access by faith into this grace wherein we stand, and rejoice in hope of the glory of God. —Rom 5:2

These two verses give us different perspectives on **the state of existence, and how it is accessed** by those who embrace the gospel through faith, it is powerful, intense, glorious, and it is NOW a reality!

...by one, Jesus Christ.

Jesus Christ is the only means to this power and possession. *(Compare the following verses with this chapters title page 88.)*

> And when he had taken the book, the four beasts and four and twenty elders fell down before the Lamb, having every one of them harps, and golden vials full of incenses, which are the prayers of saints. And they sung a new song, saying, Thou art worthy to take the book, and to open the seals thereof: for thou wast slain, and hast redeemed us to God by thy blood out of every kindred, and tongue, and people, and nation; And **hast made us** unto our God kings and priests: and we shall reign on the earth. —Rev 5:8,9

And we **do reign!** Because the territory we now possess was once under the reign of mighty Death. It's ok to do a little dance right were you are and rejoice in this cosmos shaking truth!

As we have been born the offspring of Adam, we have now become the offspring of God through Jesus:

> Blessed be the God and Father of our Lord Jesus Christ, who hath blessed us with all spiritual blessings in heavenly places in Christ: According as he hath chosen us in

him before the foundation of the world, that we should be holy and without blame before him in love: Having predestinated us unto the adoption of children by Jesus Christ to himself, according to the good pleasure of his will, —Eph 1:3 -5

Now we have learned through v. 17 all that v. 15 means.

Summary

But not as the offence, so also is the free gift. **(For if through the offence of one many be dead, much more the grace of God, and the gift by grace, which is by one man, Jesus Christ, hath abounded unto many.)** — Rom. 5:15

- After stating emphatically that the comparison between Adam and Jesus is negative and not positive, verse 15b is the **first proof** that the free gift of the one man Jesus is not like the offense of the one man Adam.
- The comparison is between the source of life and that of death. Through Adam's offense Death reigned, through Jesus' gift of righteousness Life reigns.
- "Much more the grace of God..."; *To a surpassing greater degree*, because, Death has conquered all men; Therefore, the rescue (grace) had to be **much greater**.
- The Gift": is receiving something at no cost to you. **In this letter it also describes something we could**

never afford—the price is greater than our means to pay—abundant riches given to the impoverished! This is also what grace means.

- The purpose is to establish beyond a doubt, that the one man Jesus Christ can reconcile us to God, and save us from the wrath of God which is to come *(5:10)*; Therefore, the repetition of *one* and *many*.

- **Hath Abounded**, is equal to my idea of *Overkill*. It means to excel or super abound—over-kill gives the correct sense of *even greater* force over the offense and Death—it is excessive force. This word will be used again at the end of chapter five to summarize the whole teaching!

- **v.17** is the parallel to 15b. *For if by one man's offense death reigned [to rule as king] by one; much more [to a greater degree] they which receive [to take] abundance [superabundant, superior, preeminence] of grace and of the gift of righteousness shall reign in life by one, Jesus Christ.*

- One man's offense... The offense is the disobedience of Adam in the garden of Eden.

- This verse gets to the title of our book: It highlights a striking defeat and transfer of POWER: Death reigned as king over all of humanity, yet, its reign was supplanted, over-ruled, by more powerful kings—*US!* We who lay hold of super abundance of grace and righteousness through Jesus Christ—we reign in LIFE!

- Verses 15 and 1,2 give us different perspectives on **the state of existence** (compare 5:1-2), for those who embrace the gospel through faith, it is powerful, intense, and glorious.

So, the first proof that Jesus is not like Adam, but is much greater, is because the gift of righteousness, which comes through him, is much more powerful than Death, that came through Adam.

As we move on to the next proof, let's keep in mind, that these varied aspects and perspectives of our life in Christ are given so that we can appreciate all of the ingredients that make this dynamite (power) the greatest force we know of in creation, and that we will not be ashamed of it:

> For I am not ashamed of the gospel of Christ: for it is the power of God unto salvation to every one that believeth; to the Jew first, and also to the Greek. —Rom 1:16

Ashamed?

Are you ashamed of the gospel that some people call a foolish fantasy? (2Cor. 1) It takes the New Birth to see the kingdom of God:

> Jesus answered and said unto him, Verily, verily, I say unto thee, Except a man be born again, he cannot see the kingdom of God. —Joh 3:3

Once you are re-born to see its reality, you will never be ashamed of the POWER it takes to free you from God's wrath, Sin, and Death, and provide entrance into this domain of grace.

Knowledge and persuasion remove shame!

> 2Ti 1:12 for which cause also these things I suffer, but I am not ashamed, **for I have known** in whom I have believed, and have been persuaded that he is able to keep that which I have committed to him to guard-- to that day.

How could Paul feel shame when he was sent by the Lord who proved his power over these forces by the resurrection?

> Rom 1:3 Concerning his Son Jesus Christ our Lord, which was made of the seed of David according to the flesh; And declared to be the Son of God with power, according to the spirit of holiness, by the resurrection from the dead: By whom we have received grace and apostleship, for obedience to the faith among all nations, for his name:

This study in Romans 5 is designed to persuade us:

> And hope maketh not ashamed; because the love of God is shed abroad in our hearts by the Holy Ghost which is given unto us. —Rom 5:5

Keep studying until God's truths become more real than the earthly things your natural eyes see.

Proof 2: Acquittal is Much Better than Condemnation

Even as also David says of the blessedness of the man to whom God counts righteousness apart from works: "Blessed are those whose lawlessnesses are forgiven, and whose sins are covered; blessed the man to whom the Lord will in no way charge sin." — Rom 4:6-8

And not as it was by one that sinned, so is the gift: for the judgment was by one to condemnation, but the free gift is of many offenses unto justification —Rom. 5:16

Lit. trans.: *And the gift is not as through one having sinned; for indeed the judgment was out of one to condemnation, but the free gift is out of many deviations to justification.*

...And not [absolute negative] **as it was by** [dia: through; channel—not cause] **one that sinned, so is the gift...**

RWP:..."Through one having sinned." That is Adam. Another contrast, difference in source (ek).

This is his **second and final proof** that the free gift is absolutely not like the offense. The typology between Adam and Jesus is negative not positive. Notice that our attention is directed through Adam, not "in" him—Adam was the channel.

...for the judgment [legal decision] **was by** [ek: out of, away from] **one, to** [indicating the point reached or entered] **condemnation** [adverse, guilty sentence],

but the free gift is of *[ek: out of, away from]* **many offenses unto** *[to, indicating the point reached or entered]* **justification** *[righteousness, favorable judgment by which God acquits.]*

> RWP: Of many trespasses …The gift by Christ grew out of manifold sins by Adam's progeny.

To understand this verse, we must have the picture of a court room in our mind. A judge on the bench (God), a standard of law, the accused (us), and a sentence declared. It is this kind of changing of symbolism that makes it difficult to follow and understand the teaching, and properly interpret the scriptures. Nevertheless it's God's way, so lets persevere.

Verses 15 & 17 focused on the accused sinners and the affect of Adam's crime on everyone—the sentence of **Death**; Contrasted with the gift of righteousness through Jesus Christ, and its affect on many—the gift of **Life**.

Our current verses, 16 & 18 focus on the sentence/judgment *out from* Adam, resulting in **Condemnation** upon all men. Contrasted with **Justification** (verdict of righteous, not guilty!) *out from* many crimes resulting in **Life (v 18)** that came upon all men.

The comparison is between condemnation and justification. It is the verb *"ek"—out from,* which controls the action and points us toward the focus of this flashback: the legal sentence—**The verdict of acquittal resulting in life, because of righteous, is better than guilt and condemnation.**

The picture is **judicial**—this verse is the first use of the word **condemnation** in this letter, and foreshadows the familiar *"There is therefore now no condemnation to those who are in Christ..."* in chapter 8:1. It also takes us back to the wrath of the judge upon the guilty:

> For God's wrath is revealed from Heaven on all ungodliness and unrighteousness of men, holding the truth in unrighteousness,
> —Rom 1:18

...for the judgment was by one to condemnation...but the free gift is of [from, out of, away from] **many offenses**

The truth in this verse has already been confirmed in Chapters 1-3 of this letter, where the *many sins/crimes* of mankind where listed and charged, resulting in condemnation (3:9, 19), followed by a declaration that ***out of*** this condition of worldwide condemnation, the righteousness of God ***to*** all who believe is revealed. *Note that Adam is never mentioned in the first 3 chapters <u>as the cause</u> of mankind's guilt before God (another blow to "federal imputation"):*

> Now we know that what things soever the law saith, it saith to them who are under the law: that every mouth may be stopped, and **all the world may become guilty before God...But now the righteousness of God** without the law is manifested, being witnessed by the law and the prophets; Even the **righteousness of God** which is by faith

> of Jesus Christ unto **all** and upon **all** them *that believe*: for there is no difference: For **all have sinned**, and come short of the glory of God; Being **justified freely** by his **grace** through the redemption that is in Christ Jesus: —**Rom 3:19-24**

The difference between chapters 3 and 5 is: now he shows the POWER it took to provide the free gift of righteousness/justification. (Also note, righteousness is not automatic or universal, but upon **all** *who have faith.* "All" doesn't always mean every human being without exception. The context determines who it refers to; So here, it is "the whole" of a certain group — FAITHers.)

Additionally, verse 25 of Chapter 3 also includes the idea of justification coming *out of* many trespasses:

> Whom God hath set forth to be a propitiation through faith in his blood, to declare his **righteousness** for the remission of **sins** that are past, through the forbearance of God; —**Rom 3:25**

"Sins that are past" being the reason for the propitiatory work of Christ. Hence, the free gift of righteousness was born **out of many past trespasses/crimes**—deliberate violations of prohibitions or innate knowledge of right and wrong discussed in chapter 1 of Romans. (see also 3;9-20 for a list of humanity's crimes.)

For those who want to understand "propitiation": It denotes *a satisfactory payment* for—in this case—**crimes against God,** so as to turn away [appease/satisfy] His wrath and punishment. In the past God may have appeared passive, by threatening punishment but not delivering for each crime—He was forbearing up until Christ's death. —Rom. 3:25)

> For the wrath of God **is revealed** from heaven against <u>all ungodliness and unrighteousness of men</u>, who hold the truth in unrighteousness;—Rom 1:18

...but the free gift is of many offenses *unto justification*

Justification is **the** opposite of condemnation. It is a legal state and verdict of "acquittal/no condemnation". In the NT, this state of justification is realized because the person is declared righteous, **having fulfilled all the requirements of the law**—they are righteous/justified. This is amazing because the righteousness is IMPUTED—not earned. In other words the justified person is actually guilty according to his deeds.

> For what saith the scripture? Abraham believed God, and it **was counted** unto him for righteousness. Now to him that worketh is the reward not reckoned of grace, but of debt. But to him that worketh not, but believeth on him that justifieth the ungodly, **his faith is counted for righteousness.** —Rom 4:3-5

(We will see this truth developed as we go forward in Romans.)

Out of **many offenses** the free gift results in acquittal on the basis of righteousness—this is grace!

Original Sin In This Verse

This verse argues against the idea of "original sin:" or the idea *the whole world sinned "in" Adam*. Which would mean, all mankind *essentially* committed the exact sin of Adam, at the exact same time Adam did. This would mean: instead of *"the one that sinned"* it should read "the many that sinned". And instead of justification being *"out of many transgressions"* it would be *out of one transgression*.

Some teach **the free gift of righteousness** has *in view* the many *future offenses* of Christians. But, the word used here clearly means the many offenses were the **source** (originating cause) of the free gift, just as the one offense was the source (originating cause) of the judgment. So we are to look back not forward to future sins.

All proof about mankind's guilt and condemnation was established in chapters 1-3 as absolute fact, proved by detailing their many sins.

> What then? are we better than they? No, in no wise: for we have before proved both Jews and Gentiles, that they are all under sin; As it is written, There is none righteous, no, not one: There is none that understandeth, there is none that seeketh after God. They are all gone out of the way, they are together become unprofitable; there is none that doeth good, no, not one. Their throat is an open sepulchre; with their tongues they have used deceit; the poison of asps is under their lips Whose mouth is full of cursing

and bitterness: Their feet are swift to shed blood: Destruction and misery are in their ways: And the way of peace have they not known: There is no fear of God before their eyes. Now we know that what things soever the law saith, it saith to them who are under the law: that every mouth may be stopped, and all the world may become guilty before God. Therefore by the deeds of the law there shall no flesh be justified in his sight: for by the law is the knowledge of sin. **—Rom 3:9-20**

The beginning of chapter 5 also focuses on the sinful condition of those God set his love upon. Adam as the cause of men's **personal guilt** is never mentioned—everyone is *condemned* for their own sins—*"many offences"*. Sin entered the world through Adam, then it was repeated by everyone else. Now to v. 18 for the fuller explanation of v. 16.

Rom 5:18 Therefore *[So then]***, as by** *[through]* **the offense** *[to deviate from truth/law]* **of one came upon** *[ice, to or into, indicating the point reached or entered]* **all men to condemnation** *[adverse/ guilty sentence]***; even so** *[in the same way]* **by** *[through]* **the righteousness of one the free gift came upon** *[same as above]* **all men unto** *[same as above]* **justification of life.**

Lit: So then, as through one deviation it was toward all men to condemnation, so also through one righteous act toward all men to justification of life.

RWP: So then (ara oun). Conclusion of the argument. Cf. Rom_7:3, Rom_7:25; Rom_8:12, etc. Paul resumes the parallel between Adam and Christ begun in verse Rom_5:12 and interrupted by explanation (Rom_5:13 f.) and contrast (Rom_5:15- 17).

Robertson's Word Pictures, like some commentaries, believe the comparison between Adam and Jesus was meant to be exact "parallel", so they see the intervening verses as an interruption, and the exact comparison is now picked back up. I hope I have demonstrated that this interpretation is unnecessary, because the Spirit of God never meant the type to be an exact harmony—There is no interruption in thought in this passage. The so-called "interruption" is necessary so that we don't make the mistake of believing the figure/type is exact parallel; but understand that it's a comparison of opposites.

by one offense: *[trespass of Adam.]* **came upon** *[eis, to or into, indicating the point reached or entered]* **all men to condemnation**

My Note: Through Adam's trespass, **judgment** *(not in the original: added by translators)*, sin **reached all men** which led to condemnation. (If it was "imputed in Adam" the judgment would not have had to travel anywhere.) The emphasis of verse 16 was out from a source to a destination. Here the focus is the channel through which it traveled and the destination reached.

even so [in the same way] **by** *[through]* **the righteousness of one the free gift came upon** *[eis]* **all men unto justification of life.**

"Even So" compares the effects of the offense on the "all men" to the righteous act of one "upon all men", for the purpose of assuring the "faithful" that all men can be/and are accounted righteous, and have life through faith in "one man".

One act of righteousness (a more accurate translation) likely refers to Rom. 3:22 if *"faith of Jesus Christ"* is properly translated *"faithfulness of Jesus Christ"*, referring to his **perfect obedience** to the Father unto death on the cross, resulting in him being declared righteousness. **The next verse confirms "obedience" is the one act referred to.** When we get there we'll discuss more details.

RWP: Through one act of righteousness. That of Christ. The first "unto all men" as in verse Rom_5:12, the second as in verse Rom_5:17 "they that receive, etc."

The first "all men" should not cause us to ignore the **"many" which is used 3 times as often** in the preceding verses. All=Many. Since Paul is closing, his argument he is likely emphasizing the full extent of power, as the next verses will show. All human beings without exception are NOT justified, only "the many" as we have seen. **But ALL of the faith-full are justified—the whole group!** *(Refer back to "Many offenses" on pages 108-109.)*

Once again we see the legal setting: justification leads to acquittal/no condemnation and therefore LIFE! And LIFE through Jesus's act of obedience is far better than condemnation from Adam's transgression! (cp. v. 11)

Summary

And not as it was by [through] one that sinned, so is the gift: for the judgment [verdict] was by [out of] one to condemnation, but the free gift is of [out of] many offenses unto justification...Therefore as by the offence of one judgment came upon all men to condemnation; even so by the righteousness of one the free gift came upon all men unto justification of life. —**Rom. 5:16,18**

- This is the **second and final proof** that Adam **is not exactly like Jesus**—they are a "figure/type" of contrast. This is a LEGAL SETTING—picture a court room trial.
- Verses 15 & 17 focused on the accused sinners and the affect of Adam's crime on everyone—the sentence of **Death**, contrasted with the gift of righteousness through Jesus Christ, and its affect on many—which is the gift of **Life**. Our current verses, 16 & 18 focus on the comparison between condemnation and justification —the verdict. It is the verb *"ek"—out from,* which points us toward (eis) the focus of this flashback: the legal sentence:: **righteous acquittal and life is better than a guilty verdict and condemnation.**
- The truth in these verses has already been confirmed in Chapters 1-3 of this letter, where the *many sins/ crimes* of mankind where listed and charged, resulting in condemnation (3:9—19), followed by a declaration that *out of* this condition of worldwide condemnation, the righteousness of God *to* all who believe is revealed:
- Although chapters 3 and our current verses establish the guilt of mankind before God, based on their sins, the difference between chapters 3 and 5 is, now we are shown the POWER it took to provide the free gift of righteousness/justification through faith.
- These verses argue against the idea of "original sin:" or *the whole world sinned "in" Adam.* Which would mean all mankind *essentially* committed the exact sin of Adam, at the exact same time Adam did. This

would mean that instead of *"the one that sinned"* it should read "the many that sinned". And instead of justification being *out of many transgressions,* it would be *out of one transgression.*

- Through Adam's trespass, **judgment <u>reached all men,</u>** which led to condemnation. If it was "imputed in Adam" the judgment would not have had to travel anywhere.

- The emphasis of verse 16 was ***out from*** a source to the **destination**. In verse 18 the focus is the channel ***through*** which it ***traveled to the destination***—the destinations are condemnation and righteousness and life—THE FINAL LEGAL VERDICTS!

The Verdict of Acquittal, resulting in Life, is Much Better than the Sentence of Condemnation, and **the one man Jesus is therefore greater** than the one man Adam.

End of the Typology

> For as by one man's disobedience many were made sinners, so, by the obedience of one shall many be made righteous.
> — Rom 5:19

For as by one man's disobedience...

P aul is now reviewing and summarizing the details of the flashbacks to Adam and Jesus. He is making sure his whole teaching on Adam being a figure of Christ is understood.

It all comes down to one man, one act— Adam's **disobedience**, and Jesus **obedience**. Obedience means to pay attention to a rule, command, or instruction. In this case, sin entered the cosmos, because Adam *failed to pay attention* to God's command not to eat of the *Tree of the Knowledge of Good and Evil*. Because Jesus's paid attention to the Father's will, many are able to be made righteous.

Through that **one disobedient act in the Garden of Eden...**

many were made [caused to be] sinners

> For *all* have sinned, and come short of the glory of God...—Rom 3:23

Chapters one through three proved that the world of men—without exception—are sinners by **practice**. Paul is now telling us the enabling **cause**—it was Adam's disobedience which made that condition possible.

This verse also takes us back to the beginning of our drama to wrap up the typology:

> Because of this, even as sin entered the world through one man, and death through sin, so also death passed to all men, in as much as **all sinned**. —Rom 5:12

Remember the use of "many" is to show how "one" can effect "many more" than himself.

> **Lit:** For as through the one man's disobedience the many were constituted sinners, so also through the obedience of the One the many shall be constituted righteous.

The word *made or constituted* simply refers to the effect of Adams sin—the **means by which** many were made sinners was shown in the first three chapters of this letter. It was basically summarized in chapter one verse 18 as *suppressing the truth*.

Made Means Imputed?

"Made" does not mean imputed. If "imputation" was intended, the preposition "in" would have been used *(as it is in many places. eg. 5:1 & chp 6)*, not "through"— it would say "in one man".

If every human being born actually committed the very same sin with Adam (*"being in his loins"*), the word *imputation (Adams sin charged to the account of otherwise innocent mankind)* would also be a bad choice, because we would have committed our own individual sin along with and in him.

The idea of *seminal imputation* contradicts the use of the word imputation in this letter, especially as it refers to **imputed righteousness** taught in chapter 4. On account of **faith** righteousness is "imputed: graciously charged to the account" of otherwise guilty sinners, because of faith in God.

We need imputation (credit) because we cannot afford the righteousness required for life, and we have sin in our account.

> Even as David also describes the blessedness of the man, unto whom God **imputes** righteousness <u>without works,</u>—Rom 4:6

In the above verse, David was talking about receiving a direct deposit to your account in the amount sufficient to purchase eternal life and all the inheritance belonging to a son of God, **<u>without doing the required work</u>** to earn that deposit to your bank account.

Seminal imputation in Adam would be guilt charged to already guilty sinners, because we were there, not innocent souls. **This idea is illogical.**

The interpretation I am offering, agrees—not only with the first 4 1/2 chapters of this epistle—but also with the Genesis record of God's judgments against sin after the garden of Eden and before the Law. I don't recall anyone on record, except for Adam and Eve, being accused of violating the command to "*not eat of the tree in the midst of the garden*". But multitudes (even entire tribes and nations) are recorded as being judged for their own ungodliness and sins. Paul has already established this fact in chapter 1, concluding the charge of worldwide guilt in 3:9,19.

I must take a moment to re-emphasize the point that most errors in Bible interpretation occur because we get too caught up in a word or phrase, ignore the context and completely forget the information previously presented in the letter or book. How many commentaries do you notice use the context of the letter to prove their points? (I've heard some even argue against the immediate context.)

Paul told us in verse 12 how all men were made sinners: Adam was the channel through which Sin and Death entered the cosmos and subsequently passed to all men, because they too likewise sinned. One man escaped the title "sinner", that man is the One through whom righteousness comes. Adam was his father, and Jesus was in his loins—but **without sin!**

So made/constituted doesn't mean imputed; it means that the end result of Adam's disobedience was that many others became sinners like him.

by the obedience of one shall many be made righteous.

> Then said Jesus unto them, When ye have lifted up the Son of man, then shall ye know that I am he, and that I do nothing of myself; but as my Father hath taught me, I speak these things. And he that sent me is with me: the Father hath not left me alone; **for I do always those things that please him.** —Joh 8:28

As we saw in the last verse: the one act of righteousness is the same as the obedience described here. We know from the context the one righteous act of obedience refers specifically to Christ's Death on the cross—the topic of this chapter:

> For when we were yet without strength, in due time **Christ died for the ungodly.** For scarcely for a righteous man will one **die**: yet peradventure for a good man some would even dare to **die**. But God commendeth his love toward us, in that, while we were yet sinners, Christ **died** for us. Much more then, being now justified by his **blood**, we shall be <u>saved from wrath</u> through him. For if, when we were enemies, we were reconciled to God by the **death** of his Son, much more, being reconciled, we shall be saved by his life. And not only *so,* but we also joy in God through our Lord Jesus

> Christ, by whom we have now received the atonement. —Rom 5:6-11

> Who, being in the form of God, thought it not robbery to be equal with God: But made himself of no reputation, and took upon him the form of a servant, and was made in the likeness of men: And being found in fashion as a man, he humbled himself, and became **obedient unto death, even the death of the cross.** —Php 2:6ff

The picture here is profound! Jesus' horrific death represented incomprehensible obedience and sacrifice. It will likely take the enlightenment of heaven for us to comprehend how a perfect God would accept the humiliation of becoming a created thing, and the vulnerability of birth and infancy, suffer his own terrible wrath to the fullest, to wholeheartedly accept to himself corrupt beings as natural born sons, equal to the obedient One.

Hebrews gives a closer look at Jesus' obedience and his expectation:

> Looking unto Jesus…who for the joy that was set before him endured the cross, despising the shame, and is set down at the right hand of the throne of God. —Heb 12:2

many be made [same as above] *righteous.*

This verse says nothing of our *union with* Adam or Christ, but, of the effects to the human race *through* each of them. (This is a very common mistake: as we teachers impose our knowledge of our "union with Christ" into every passage.)

According to the previous 2 chapters of Romans, we are accounted righteousness **on the basis of belief** in God, *through* the work of Jesus—Cause and Effect, or Means and End!!

Righteousness is imputed—not because of our *union with* Christ at the cross, but is imputed *in our lifetime,* when we exercise faith…4:23-25. The Spirit of God knows the difference between the prepositional verbs *in* and *through*, and obviously uses them carefully. Chapter 6 on the other hand will emphasizes union *with* Christ in His death and resurrection—but we'll have to wait on that study.

Paraphrase:

"However, the free gift is **absolutely not** like the offence. Let me explain: If through the offence of Adam many are dead, the grace of God and the gift of righteousness, which is through Jesus Christ, is even greater, because it has overcome death to give life to many. In remarkable ways, Jesus is greater than Adam: **The first born son of God**[10] **caused condemnation and Death, the Second born Son of God ended Death's reign, giving righteousness and life to as many as receive him.** For through one man's disobedience act, many were made to be sinners, so, through the obedient act of One man many will be made righteous."

Summary

> For as by one man's disobedience many were made sinners, so, by the obedience of one shall many be made righteous. — Rom 5:19

- After providing two proofs that the typology between Adam and Jesus is **not** parallel or complimentary, and Adam is not exactly like Jesus, Paul is now reviewing and summarizing the meaning of the flashbacks to Adam and Jesus. He is making sure his whole teaching on Adam being a figure of Christ is understood.

- Obedience means to pay attention to a rule, command, or instruction—Adam was disobedient, Jesus paid full attention to God the Father.

- *"many where made sinners"* explains verse 12 and chapter 3:23 which states: "all have sinned". So, the affect of one man's disobedience was that many others also became sinners.

- "Made" does not mean imputed (credited to the account). If "imputation" was intended, the verse would read "**in** one man's disobedience many were made sinners". *Seminal imputation* in Adam would be guilt credited to already guilty sinners (because they were there), not innocent souls. ***This idea is illogical.***

- So, made/constituted doesn't mean imputed; it means that **the end result** of Adam's disobedience was that many others became sinners like him.

- We know from the context, the "one righteous act of obedience" refers specifically to Christ's Death on the cross—which is the topic of chapter 5:
- Righteousness is imputed—not because of our *union with* Christ at the cross, but is imputed when we exercise faith…4:23-25, So "made righteous" means became righteous.

Final Flashbacks 3: Law Empowers Sin

Grace Over-Kills through Jesus Christ!

Moreover the law entered, that the offence might abound. But where Sin abounded, grace did much more abound: That [so] as Sin hath reigned unto death, even so might Grace reign through righteousness unto eternal life by Jesus Christ our Lord.—Rom 5:20-21

Now we have come to the final flashbacks in history

Moreover...

Moreover is a kind of "but wait there's more" conjunction. It can indicate either adversative (but) or continuative (additional) information is to follow. I believe the above translation has it correct, highlighting that even more spectacular events in this story of CONQUEST are to come—the last two remarkable flashbacks to the greatest war in world history:

1. The Law's arrival.
2. The **super**-conquest of Grace!

...the *law entered, that the offense might abound*

Now that the contrast between Adam and Christ is closed: Sin and Death have been CONQUERED by Righteousness and Life, we must address the last opposing King—the Law. Since it was a very important opposing player in the drama, it is spotlighted. In verse 13 our attention was directed from Adam up to the Law, now...

The Law takes center stage in our drama.

The word *law* in the original text is without the definite article "the". It simply says "law entered". We know by the context the reference is to the Law of Moses. This is a historical fact! There was no set of written laws from God given to any person or group before Moses. The fact that it was written also marks its entrance into the world and puts it on permanent record.

It was the only law given to men until Jesus:

> A <u>new commandment</u> I give unto you, That ye love one another; as I have loved you, that ye also love one another.—Joh 13:34

entered: *(to come in alongside, that is, supervene. By stealth.)*

Entered alongside means: it had a supportive role to Sin and Death. It also implies it's intention was not obviously recognizable—it entered by stealth or secretly.

Laws timetable in the history of redemption.

> For until the law sin was in the world: but sin is not imputed when there is no law.—Rom 5:13

In verse 13 the focus was on Sin and Death, and their dominion from Adam to Moses. Now, Paul will tell us what happened when the Law arrived. We will learn the **effect** of imputation. *(Refer to page 54 ("Imputed") for a fuller understanding of the Law.)*

The LAW is not eternal, it had a historical beginning. It was not introduced in the garden of Eden as some say.

The ***stealth*** nature of its entry will be explained in cp. 7 (covered in the 3rd book in this series).

Law's purpose in the history of redemption.

Some falsely believe the Law came that we might have life. However, its true "stealth" purpose was: *The law came alongside so...*

that the offense:

Same word as Sin in the next sentence ("...but where *sin* abounded...")

> **VWS:** Paul replies that it came in alongside of the Sin. "It was taken up into the divine plan or arrangement, and made an occasion for the abounding of grace in the opening of the new way to justification and life" (Dwight).

How could Dwight say that the appearance of The Law "made an occasion for the abounding of grace," when the scripture clearly says the purpose was *"that the offense may abound"*?

The Law's appearance was like a city posting signs in a school zone because drivers are speeding around all those children. Once the signs go up, the fines go up. When the Law is posted, offenses increase. (Now, we know the abounding of grace is coming, but let's not jump ahead and miss the present scene in this dramatic flashback.)

This error happens when men are hasty to dismiss any suggestion that the Law was a negative influence in the world.

The word *offense* is singular, so as to emphasize the personal benefit that SIN (Offense), the Conquering King, received by the Law. The Offense (Sin)...

might abound:

It's (the Offense's) POWER and TERRITORY increased! This is an important word picture, meant to intensify the drama.

> **Thayer:** 1a) of things; 1a1) to exist in abundance; 1a2) **to increase,** 1a3) **be augmented**

This verse completely harmonizes with Paul's previous discussion about Sin and the Law's relation to each other in the third chapter v. 9-21 ie.: *they are all proved under Sin, then 'it is written'*—The violations of sin preceded the Law's coming in alongside:

> ... for we have before proved both Jews and Gentiles, that they are all **under sin**; As **it is written**, There is none righteous, no, not one...Now we know that what things soever the law saith, it saith to them who are **under the law**: that every mouth may be stopped, and all the world may **become guilty before God.** —Rom 3:9-19

The Law is introduced for official, legal guilt/sin. (Mankind is pictured as *under* the reign of Sin, and later the Law also.) Under the Law, offenses increase; and are more clearly defined. It's like shining a light in a completely dark and dusty room. *(Paul gives even greater detail on this relationship in chapter 7.)* And some people wonder why Moses' Law was so detailed and graphic—it covered all sins wherever they existed, so as to cause Sin to abound. (compare Gal. 3:19-25)

This abounding of Sin, also explains how God's **righteousness comes out of many offenses unto justification (v.**

16b). The Laws purpose was to increase the presence, power, proliferation, and the reign of Sin. By the time Jesus (Righteousness) arrived, the history and public record of men's sins was abundant—as Rom. 3:9-20 details.

> But Law came in besides, that the deviation might abound. —Rom 5:20

> But before faith came, we were kept under the law, shut up unto the faith which should afterwards be revealed. —Gal 3:23

> The sting (poison) of Death *is* Sin; and the strength [power] of Sin *is* the Law. —1Cor. 15:56

The poison that causes Death is Sin, and the strength of that poison, is the Law. The Law increased the potency of the poison called Sin. In real life, it broadened Sin's territory by reaching into the heart/motives as well as the actions of mankind—"love God with all your heart, and your neighbor as yourself." **Thereby, the Law became a powerful friend for Sin.**

Now for the second "Moreover" and last flashback:

Can I remind you that we are not reading creative poetry, but are being given insight into super-natural realities!

> For all things are for your sakes, that the abundant grace might through the thanksgiving of many redound to the glory of

> God... While we look not at the things which are seen, but at the things which are not seen: for the things which are seen are temporal; but the things which are not seen are eternal. —2Co 4:15

Flashback 4: Grace Over-kills

But *[moreover]* where Sin abounded,

"Moreover:" This phrase introduces a kind of "if you thought that was an incredible event, you've got to see this!" There is an incredible excerption to Sin's conquest in 33 AD when Christ died and rose from the grave. **In the very same territory where Sin abounded/conquered and established its throne...**

Grace did much more abound:

Grace super-abounded! **Where Sin conquered, Grace over-conquered!** This phrase takes us back to the first 11 verses of Romans 5, and Jesus's conquest. The drama opened with our entrance into "this grace in which we stand"; it now closes with a celebration of the conquest that made this entrance possible.

> Therefore being justified by faith...we have access by faith **into this grace wherein we**

stand, and rejoice in hope of the glory of God. —Rom 5:1

It also mirrors *that "super abundance of grace and righteousness"* taken possession of by faithful believers:

...much more they which receive **abundance of grace** and of the gift of righteousness shall reign in life by one, Jesus Christ. Rom 5:17

Lit: *Moreover Law came in besides, that the deviation might abound. But where Sin abounded, grace much more abounded,*

"So" that there is no doubt about how this entire drama ends and what it means, the last verse sums it up…

That** [so] **as Sin has reigned unto** [destination] **death, even so** [n the same way, in the same territory] **might grace reign through righteousness unto** [destination] **eternal life by Jesus Christ our Lord.

RWP: That—**even so grace might reign**. Final here, the purpose of God and the goal for us through Christ. Lightfoot notes the force of the aorist indicative (...subjunctive (<u>...might establish its throne</u>), the ingressive aorist both times. "This full **rhetorical** (emphasis added) close has almost the value of a doxology" (Denney).

Make no mistake about it, God's purpose since Adam & Eve's sin, was to displace Sin in this cosmos, and establish Righteousness; so that Death could be replaced with Life through Jesus Christ! **"THY KINGDOM COME THY WILL BE DONE ON EARTH AS IT IS IN HEAVEN!"**

Entrance into that kingdom of God and grace is the topic of Romans 5; "Grace reigns through righteousness", *"and we being justified by faith, have peace with God through our Lord Jesus Christ: By whom also we have access by faith INTO THIS GRACE WHEREIN WE STAND, AND REJOICE IN HOPE of the glory of God. Rom 5:1,2*

Section Summary

> Moreover the law entered, that the offence might abound. But where sin abounded, grace did much more abound: That *[so]* as sin hath reigned unto death, even so might grace reign through righteousness unto eternal life by Jesus Christ our Lord.—Rom 5:20-21

- Moreover indicates even more spectacular events in this story of CONQUEST are to come.
- The LAW is not eternal, it had a historical entrance.
- ***Entered*** alongside means: the Law had a supportive role to Sin and Death. It also suggests its role was not obviously recognizable—its true mission was secret.

- **might abound:** Sin's POWER and TERRITORY INCREASED! This is an important word picture, used to intensify the drama.
- This fourth and final flashback says there is a remarkable exception to Sin's conquest. It happened in 33 AD when Christ died and rose from the grave. **In the very same territory** where Sin abounded/conquered, won its victory, Grace super-abounded! **Where Sin conquered, Grace over-conquered!**
- Some of the results of Grace's super-abounding over Sin are presented in the first 11 verses of chapter 5. The drama opened with entrance into "this grace", it now closes with a celebration of the devastating conquest that made this entrance possible.
- Grace is personified as king, because it conquered all of the opposing spiritual powers, and established its throne in the cosmos, where believers were held hostage—Grace OVERKILLED ("for by Grace you have been saved..." Eph. 2:8,9)

> That *[so]* as Sin has reigned unto Death, even so might Grace reign through righteousness unto eternal life by Jesus Christ our Lord.

Final Book Summary:

<u>OUTLINE:</u> Romans 5:12-21 is a dramatized presentation of the gospel of God's power unto salvation. It opens with a cel-

ebration of the glorious end of events—A grand entrance into a realm of bliss where all believers live!

Next, the momentous events which lead to that celebration are highlighted using 4 flashbacks. Each flashback begins with a statement of fact, followed by an explanation of historic events supporting that fact.

The final two verses return to the beginning of the drama by focusing on how Grace conquered Sin, Death, and Law, to open the door for us to enter this glorious realm where Grace now rules.

By the end of chapter 5 we have met and know the roles of the enemies/powers/rulers who stood in the way, and had to be conquered to secure our salvation, and bring us into this state of Grace. God's love not only overcame our obstinate and hardened hearts (vs 5-11), but now, we know he had to conquer our captors— Sin, Death, and Sin's Sargent at arms—the Law; to finally save us from His wrath which was revealed against us, because of our slavery and service to those powerful forces which are arrayed against him..

> For the wrath of God is revealed from heaven against all ungodliness and unrighteousness of men, who hold the truth in unrighteousness; —Rom 1:18

> But God commendeth his love toward us, in that, while we were yet sinners, Christ died for us. Much more then, being now justified by his blood, we shall be saved from wrath through him. —Rom 5:8,9

So, as it stands, Sin's powerful, devastating, world-wide reign over Believers (leading to Death) is **past tense.**

> **Even so [to the same extent, in the same territory] Grace does now reign through the gift of righteousness, leading to unending, everlasting life, through Jesus Christ our Lord.** —5:21

Verse 5:8, along with the next verses, form the reality of the believer's life, and assurance (hope 5:5) that the love of God has conquered all enemies (8:31-39)—Sin (cp.6), The Law's Condemnation (cp.7-8), Death (cps. 5, 6, 7, 8).

The word "dia" (through/by) was used 19 times in 21 verses, beginning in v.5:1 and ending in v.21. This preposition is the key to understanding the main point of the teaching in this section of the letter—it guides the drama.

The imagery presented by words such as "reign" and "super abound" are the key to understanding the meaning and interpretation of this Bible passage, as well as the next three chapters—these words personify the ruling Powers:

This passage is One Glorious, dramatic, declaration of the powerful love of God demonstrated in the life, death, and resurrection of Jesus, and the rescue of Saints through faith.

<u>Adam was **the one**</u> through whom these enemies entered the world and gained ruling power.

<u>Jesus Christ is **the One**</u> through whom *all obstacles and enemies* between God and those He loves, have been once-for-all removed, and a permanent state of grace and life established. All of this we have access to *by* faith (5:2ff). Supernatu-

ral faith and the awareness of God's love, is THE PROOF that the Holy Spirit has birthed us into this reality!

Finally, this doctrinal drama is not non-fiction; It is a window into spiritual realities our earthly eyes cannot see, but we profess to see when we believe the gospel of salvation.

> For our citizenship is in Heaven, from where we also wait for a Savior, the Lord Jesus Christ, who will transform our body of humiliation, for it to be conformed to His body of glory, according to the working of Him to be able even to subject all things under Himself.—Php 3:20,21

Coming Attractions...

Beginning with chapter 6, Paul will add to, and expand upon the facts he has just established, by showing in detail, **how** every enemy has been conquered by Jesus Christ on our behalf, and the spiritual and practical benefits accruing to us rescued believers.

We might consider the deception, hostility, slavery, murder, rescue, love and forgiveness, we've just witnessed in chapter five as an epic trailer...an overview...coming attractions, and the next three chapters, the main event—the full featured block buster documentary of the momentous world changing events.

So now you know the truth of the gospel of faith, and how it came to be—next the rescue, **how** it happened, and the aftermath.

And I heard a loud voice saying in heaven, Now is come salvation, and strength, and the kingdom of our God, and the power of his Christ —Rev 12:10

And the seventh angel sounded; and there were great voices in heaven, saying, The kingdoms of this world are become *the kingdoms* of our Lord, and of his Christ; and he shall reign for ever and ever. — Rev 11:15

AMEN!

The End of chapter 5

Appendix

The Love of God

As the motivation for rescue can't be overlooked or minimized: We are told it was the REASON God purposed, planned, and executed the salvation of many captives—it was because He loved them, and wanted them to enjoy life and fellowship with Him for all eternity, and not to become victims of His wrath and death.

It was more than mercy and pity…it was personal…it was love. **Agape, the love drawn out because of the value/worth of the object the love is set upon.**

Joh 3:16 For God so loved the world that He gave His only-begotten Son, that whoever believes in Him should not perish but have everlasting life.

Now we know more of the power and extent of God's love for the world.

We will cover this key doctrine of God's love when we wrap this series up in chapter 8—stay tuned!

The Powerful Strategy and Method of Rescue:

Here are a few more verses that shed light on the power of God unto salvation we've been studying.

Mat 12:28-29 But if I cast out devils by the Spirit of God, then the kingdom of God is come unto you. Or else how can one enter into a strong man's house, and spoil his goods, except he first bind the strong man? and then he will spoil his house.

Joh 12:28-32 Father, glorify thy name. Then came there a voice from heaven, saying, I have both glorified it, and will glorify it again. The people therefore, that stood by, and heard it, said that it thundered: others said, An angel spake to him. Jesus answered and said, This voice came not because of me, but for your sakes. Now is the judgment of this world: now shall the prince of this world be cast out. And I, if I be lifted up from the earth, will draw all men unto me.

Hostages led to freedom:

> Eph 4:8-10 Wherefore he saith, When he ascended up on high, he led captivity captive, and gave gifts unto men. (Now that he ascended, what is it but that he also descended first into the lower parts of the earth? He that descended is the same also that ascended up far above all heavens, that he might fill all things.)

The passage above is frequently misinterpreted to refer to Jesus descending into Hell after his death. However, in light of our study, it is easy to see that it simply describes his leaving heaven above to accomplish redemption on earth. Compare the above passage to:

> Php 2:6 Who, being in the form of God, thought it not robbery to be equal with God: But made himself of no reputation, and took upon him the form of a servant, and was made in the likeness of men: And being found in fashion as a man, he humbled himself, and became obedient unto death, even the death of the cross. Wherefore God

also hath highly exalted him, and given him a name which is above every name:

Mat 6:13 And lead us not into temptation, but deliver us from evil: For thine is the kingdom, and the power, and the glory, for ever. Amen.

Rom 7:24 O wretched man that I am! who shall deliver me from the body of this death? I thank God through Jesus Christ our Lord...

Heb 2:14 Forasmuch then as the children are partakers of flesh and blood, he also himself likewise took part of the same; that through death he might destroy him that had the power of death, that is, the devil; And deliver them who through fear of death were all their lifetime subject to bondage.

1Cor 15:24-27 Then cometh the end, when he shall have delivered up the kingdom to God, even the Father; when he shall have put down all rule and all authority and power. For he must reign, till he hath put all enemies under his feet. The last enemy that shall be destroyed is death. For he hath put all things under his feet.

A Law Before Moses?

Why would some teachers commit the error of adding "a law" between Adam and Moses (5:14)?

> Nevertheless death reigned from Adam to Moses, even over them that had not sinned after the similitude of Adam's transgression, who is the figure of him that was to come. —Rom 5:14

Why would some teachers distort the picture of history Paul is presenting here? It can be summed up in a phrase *self righteous legalism*: the need to appear holy before God in one's self. You might say, this is the story of the New Testament. It was the bases of the opposition Jesus received from the religious leaders of his day, and the Apostle's persecutions from the same group of religious leaders recorded in Acts and the epistles. Paul summarizes the mindset like this:

> For I bear them record that they have a zeal of God, but not according to knowledge. For they being ignorant of God's righteousness, and going about to establish their own righteousness, have not submitted themselves unto the righteousness of God. For Christ *is* the end of the law for righteousness to everyone that believeth.—**Rom. 10:2-4**

The overwhelming need of legalist to make **grace subject to Law,** by insisting on the law's *eternal dominion,* is destructive to the gospel. But, the legalist, ***disbelieving*** that God can impute righteousness by faith, without law-mandated works, insist that the Law is eternal, therefore obedience to its commands are mandatory—forever! **To prove this, they must interpret Romans 5:14 in a way that removes the *time frame* of the Laws <u>entrance</u> into the world. They insist the totality of the law of Moses was given to Adam in the garden and it was not abolished by Christ's death**—it is eternal! This as we have seen is poor interpretation and false doctrine.

More Answers to the Objections of Legalist

Now, popular questions about the Law and the gospel of Faith.

Legalist Objectors insist:

Objection. There can be no grace without first receiving the law.

Answer. In chapter 4 Paul hammers home the fact that Abraham was justified by faith, **as a Gentile**—before there was a law of Moses. So a Gentile was pronounced righteous by grace through faith, without the law. (This fact destroys legalism!)

> How was it then reckoned? when he was in circumcision, or in uncircumcision? Not in circumcision, but in uncircumcision. And he received the sign of circumcision, a seal of the righteousness of the faith which *he had yet* being uncircumcised: that he might be the father of all them that believe, **though they be not circumcised;**

that righteousness might be imputed unto them also: And the father of circumcision to them who are not of the circumcision only, but who also walk in the steps of that faith of our father Abraham, which *he had being yet* uncircumcised. For the promise, that he should be the heir of the world, *was* **not to Abraham, or to his seed, through the law**, but through the righteousness of faith.—**Rom 4:10-13**

O. The Law is a reflection of the nature of God, and is therefore eternal.

A. True, the law is a reflection of the nature of God (*"Be ye holy, for I am Holy"*). However, there is no scripture which teaches it is eternal. In fact, the law of Moses/God clearly entered human history when it was given to Moses—just as our text says. There is no contradiction or confusion between the Old Testament historical record and the words of Paul in this passage. In fact, the **New Covenant promise** was that the *external* commandments contained in the Law would be unnecessary:

> But this *shall be* the covenant that I will make with the house of Israel; After those days, saith the LORD, I will put my law in their inward parts, and write it in their hearts; and will be their God, and they shall be my people. And they shall teach no more every man his neighbor, and every man his brother, saying, Know the LORD: for they shall all know me, from the least of them

unto the greatest of them, saith the LORD: for I will forgive their iniquity, and I will remember their sin no more. —Jer 31:33

It is amazing that legalist would ignore this promise which was fulfilled in Acts, and insist that we still need to enforce the Law of Commandments given through Moses.

Additionally, *"Christ is the **end** of the law for righteousness to everyone that believeth."* *(Rom.10)* Anything with an "end" is not "eternal," but is temporary. Some argue that the end is only pertaining to righteousness, but it is still necessary as a "guide". A guide to what if not righteousness or right living? This reasoning doesn't make sense.

O. All men—including Christians—are bound to keep the law of God/Moses.

A. Paul has clearly stated before in: **Rom 3:21-22**

But now the righteousness of God **without the law** is manifested, being witnessed by the law and the prophets; Even the righteousness of God which is by faith of Jesus Christ unto all and upon all them that believe: for there is no difference:

Righteousness of God **is not in any way** tied to the law, believers therefore, cannot be bound by it as legalist insist.

O. This Romans passage (5:14) can't teach that there was a time when the world was without the law of God, because sin is essentially a transgression of the law of God. No Law = No Sin.

A. As we have seen, Sin existed before the Law, so it's not dependant on the Law for its existence, as Paul demonstrated in the beginning of his letter:

> "For the wrath of God is revealed from heaven against all ungodliness and unrighteousness of men, who hold (suppress) the truth in unrighteousness; Because that which may be known of God is manifest in them; for God hath showed it unto them."
> —**Rom 1:18-19**

Here the sin is not a violation of God's written law, but a **suppression of innate** *(God given)* **knowledge.** The definition of sin in this passage is a malfunction: God implanted knowledge that should have produced glory and praise from men to Him their creator. Instead, that truth was suppressed and not allowed to produce its intended results. It was replaced by error, or glory and praise for created things.

So Paul, in Romans 1, has already given "sin" another definition than *transgressing* the Law of Moses.

Finally: The story of the New Testament is ***all about*** the transition from God dealing with a single nation, with whom he had a legal covenant, to saving all nations by grace through faith (through a New Covenant). Therefore, these answers to the objections of legalist are a small portion of what the New Testament has to say against them.

Here is our paraphrase one more time:

> **Paraphrase *v. 14:*** Notwithstanding there <u>not</u> being the Law, or the imputation of sin...**Death reigned as dictatorial King**

from Adam to Moses, even over them that had not *sinned* equivalent to Adam's transgression.

End Notes

[1] Vincent's Word Studies, Robertson Word Pictures and Albert Barnes Commentary on Romans. My emphasis on metaphorical language was learned from the Greek word studies.

[2] http://en.wikipedia.org/wiki/Overkill (term)

[3] Pavis, Shantz (1998). Dictionary of the Theatre: Terms, Concepts, and Analysis. University of Toronto Press. p. 151. ISBN 0802081630.

[4] Kenny (2004). Teaching Tv Production in a Digital World: Integrating Media Literacy. Libraries Unltd Incorporated. p. 163. ISBN 1591581990.

[5] On the use of the phrase "and so": Cp. 11:26, Matt6:9,Matt 6:30; "Likewise" Matt.17:12; "this Fashion" Mk 2:12, John 3:16 "so";John 5:26

[6] "IMPUTED" see also 7:7-10, Gal. 3:19.

[7] As far as there having to be a law during that period, consider the following: Paul has outlined, in the first chapters pages of

this letter, a most detailed account of God's wrath because of mankind's guilt and sin (summary 3:7-9), with limited and selective mention of law and several different definitions of sin:

A. According to Chapters 1-4: Death and judgment (eternal death) are the result of violating/suppressing TRUTH—1:18 , 2:8, 2:12, (3:7 truth of God) Not Law, The law is introduced as validating and establishing guilt, (through detailed commandments), confirming that all men have corrupted God's TRUTH and LIGHT and justly deserve death and condemnation (3:10-20).

B. God is Love but, He is also more than love (He is a consuming fire: Heb 12:29, He is Holy:1Pe 1:16, He is Light: 1Jo 1:5 etc.) So also Sin is a transgression of law (better translation: sin is lawlessness) but, is also more than a transgression (eg. Sin is also omission of good: the opposite of transgression!

Jam 4:17; "Whatever is not out of faith is sin"Rom.14:23, The fallen Angels sinned (2Peter2:4, Jude 1:6), they "erred" no indication that they transgressed a law.

The angels sin was most likely a violation of direct Truth and Light: Romans cp.1, That Light and Truth was obviously more brilliant for the fallen Angels; Jude 1:7: Sodom and Gomorrah are included in a list of UNGODLY SINNERS, again no biblical indication that they broke a written or spoken commandment. They along with all of the others judged in Genesis are likely included in the ungodly suppressors of truth in cp. 1:18-32)

[8] GILL: This does not exclude the dominion of death over such who had sinned after the likeness of Adam, but rather con-

firms its power over them; nor does it intend adult Gentiles, who did not sin in the same manner, nor against the same law, as Adam did; but it designs infants, not yet guilty of actual sin; and therefore since death reigns over them, who only holds and exercises his dominion by virtue of sin, it follows, that they must have original sin in them; the guilt of Adam's transgression must be imputed to them, and the corruption of nature, from him, derived unto them, or it could not reign over them. A child of a year old, the Jewish doctors say, has not tasted the taste of sin, that is, has not committed actual sin; and observe that young children die on account of the sins of their parents: but the true reason of their dying is here suggested by the apostle; which is the transgression of Adam:

[9] WHAT ABOUT INNOCENT INFANTS:

Rom 3:23 For all (adults?) have sinned, and come short of the glory of God; Compare 3:9-20, (Are infants an exception?)

Psa 51:5 Behold, I was shapen in iniquity; and in sin did my mother conceive me.) cp. Gen 8:21.

Rom 7:18 For I know that in me (that is, in my flesh), dwelleth no good thing (Was this true of the adult Paul only? Are infant's flesh good?): Rom.3:10ff

Psa 58:3 The wicked are estranged from the womb; they go astray from the belly, speaking lies. (is this hyperbole or fact?)

Hos 12:2 Jehovah also has a quarrel with Judah, and will punish Jacob according to his ways; He will repay him according to his deeds. Hos 12:3 He took his brother by the heel in the womb, and by his strength he contended with God...(Can we accept this as fact? can the unborn show such evil aggression?)

Job 25:4 How then can man be justified (righteous) with God? or how can he be clean (innocent) that is born of a woman?

Ecc 7:20 For there is not a just man upon earth, that doeth good, and sinneth not. cp. 1Kings8:46;Pro 20:9-11 (Does this exclude infants?)

[10] Luk 3:38 Which was the son of Enos, which was the son of Seth, which was the son of Adam, which was the son of God.

[11] There are compelling arguments in opposition to these however, you'll have to investigate them for yourself.

UNCONSCIOUS:
UNLOCKING THE ZONE OF EXTRAORDINARY PERFORMANCE

In *UNCONSCIOUS*, Joe Walker enters the Evolution/Atheism vs. Creation debate from a different vantage point: the perspective of super-human performance seen in athletes, musicians, geniuses, prodigies, and sudden superheroes.

Walker concludes—based on the testimony of those who have experienced the "Zone Phenomenon", the potential within our highly intelligent bodies, and the Biblical record of our creation—we are indeed *created in God's image*.

The who, what, when, why, where, and how, of this potential for extraordinary knowledge and performance are explained; As well as the road to The Zone, pitfalls, roadblocks, and much more . Finally, what does the Bible say about the future of man, and our potential to realize maximum performance?

ISBN:9780692201510
Order a copy today: http://ow.ly/vSZWw

Euthus Publishing
5300 N. Braeswood Blvd. Ste. 4151, Houston, TX 77096
1-800-405-4423
http://jwwalkerjr.com • joe@un-conscious.com

www.ingramcontent.com/pod-product-compliance
Lightning Source LLC
Chambersburg PA
CBHW071507040426
42444CB00008B/1534